Masters
of
Irish Music

Liam Gaul

NONSUCH

Frontispiece: An ancient Irish harper. This is one of John Derrick's scenes from his *Images of Ireland*, 1581.

First published 2006

Nonsuch Publishing Limited
73 Lower Leeson Street
Dublin 2
Ireland
www.nonsuch-publishing.com

British Library Cataloguing in Publication Data.
A catalogue record for this book is available from the British Library.

ISBN: 1 84588 563 5   ISBN-13: 978 184588 563 2

Typesetting and origination by Tempus Publishing Limited
Printed in Great Britain

Contents

Introduction

Ireland has a very long musical tradition stretching back over the centuries to bardic times. The harp, which also serves as our national emblem, was used by the harpers to extol the virtues of their masters. The harper occupied a special place at the chieftain's table. In *Topographia Hiberniae*, Giraldus Cambrensis gave an account of his visits to Ireland in 1183 and 1185, praising the skill of the musicians, which he said was incomparably superior to that of those of any other nation.

Turlough O'Carolan, deemed the last of the old bardic school, was a prominent exponent of the harp, as he travelled from place to place visiting and staying at the Big Houses. As a tribute to the householder he would compose a planxty or air in their honour. A large collection of Carolan's tunes set in music manuscript were published by Donal O'Sullivan in two volumes in 1958. Many of Carolan's tunes have been recorded in recent times, particularly by Derek Bell. A multi-talented musician, Bell played orchestral music for years before joining The Chieftains.

Following the Belfast Harp Festival of 1792 Edward Bunting published many of the tunes that he had been commissioned to write down by listening to the eleven harpers who participated at the festival. Thomas Moore, the poet, set many of his poems to those tunes collected and published by Bunting, thus ensuring their preservation as *Moore's Melodies*.

It was Frederick Chopin who brought the musical form of the Nocturne to prominence, but it was the Irishman John Field who invented this melodic formula and who composed a sizeable number of these tranquil melodies. Field lived mainly in Russia, where he was a piano demonstrator for Muzio Clementi.

Europe produced many operatic composers, from Bellini, Rossini and Donizetti to Mozart and Richard Wagner, adding many wonderful works to the operatic repertoire. Ireland's main operatic composers were Benedict, Balfe and

Wallace, whose three main works, *The Lily of Killarney*, *The Bohemian Girl*, and *Maritana* are collectively referred to as *The Irish Ring*. Although rarely performed today they contain many fine melodic arias, duets, and choruses.

Fine interpretations of opera require fine singing voices. This little island has produced such wonderful operatic singers as Catherine Hayes, Margaret Burke Sheridan and Dermot Troy, who graced the famed opera houses of Italy, France, England and America, singing the leading vocal roles to great critical acclaim.

In a lighter vein, Frank Patterson and John Feeney entertained presidents, monarchs and the pope with their wonderful voices. Delia Murphy, Belfast's Ruby Murray, and the red-haired Dubliner Luke Kelly brought their own brand of singing to the popular repertoire.

The most unusual, yet fascinating performer of the 1800s was Johnny Patterson, the circus clown from Feakle in County Clare. He not only composed and sang his own songs but also played the uilleann pipes, travelling America with Cooper and Bailey's Circus.

The playing of the uilleann pipes goes back a long way in Irish traditional music, with traveller pipers like Johnny Doran who attended every horse fair, race meeting and gathering throughout Ireland, where he entertained with his magical playing. 'The Steam Packet' and 'Colonel Fraser' were two of his favourite reels, which he played at great speed and yet filled with florid ornamentation and all of the piper's tricks of rolling, craning and popping.

Leo Rowsome came from a County Wexford piping dynasty that held land in the Ballintore area of Ferns. Leo was born and lived in Dublin, where he taught the uilleann pipes at the Municipal School of Music and manufactured pipes at his workshop in his home.

Seamus Ennis, as well as being a magnificent piper, was also a collector of folklore, a field in which he laboured in Ireland and England, where he presented a Sunday morning radio programme called *As I Roved Out*.

The fiddle is a very prominent instrument in Irish music, with many varying regional styles and many eminent practitioners of this art. One of the most easily identifiable was Sean Maguire, the Belfast fiddler with a unique style. Classically trained, Maguire had the added advantage of a family background of traditional music – the best of both worlds made him a very special and popular exponent of the fiddle.

The collection of our national folk music was the main interest of Captain Francis O'Neill, who was Chief of Police in Chicago. O'Neill, a native of Tralibane, County Cork, played the flute and had a store of tunes from his own area, which were recorded in manuscript form by Sergeant James O'Neill (no relation) who also served on the police force. Tunes gathered from musicians newly arrived from Ireland were amassed by Captain O'Neill and published in several volumes. This collection is just as important today as it was when first published 100 years ago.

'Boolavogue', 'Kelly the Boy from Killanne', 'Follow Me up to Carlow', and 'Sailing in the Lowlands Low' are all songs that have become part of the national song repertoire and were written by P.J. McCall. McCall was a collector, musician, poet, historian, and politician, and a Dubliner of Carlow and Wexford parentage who left a legacy of over 200 poems and recitations. He was an authority on the ancient art of mumming in south-east Wexford.

A songsmith of a different calibre was Jimmy Kennedy, who was born in Omagh, County Tyrone. Kennedy wrote popular songs including 'The Teddybears' Picnic', 'South of the Border', 'The Isle of Capri' and many, many more wonderful songs.

John Reidy – or Seán Ó'Riada, as he was later known – certainly was a master of Irish music. A native of County Limerick who studied at University College, Cork, he received great acclaim for his orchestral arrangements for George Morrison's documentary films *Mise Eire* and *Saoirse*. He incorporated some well-known traditional tunes into the scores to great effect, highlighting different aspects of the fight for Irish freedom portrayed in the black and white flickering film footage. He founded the traditional music ensemble Ceoltóirí Chualainn in which he played harpsichord and sometimes bodhrán.

One of Ireland's most eminent composers was Charles Villiers Stanford, a Dubliner born in 1852. He studied with R.M. Levey and later in London with Arthur O'Leary and Ernst Pauer. Later he became Professor of Music at Cambridge University and simultaneously Professor of Composition at the Royal College of Music. He was responsible for editing the *Complete Collection of Irish Music* by George Petrie in 1903.

Another Dubliner, Victor Herbert, was a composer of light music who was involved with orchestral and brass band music. He formed the Victor Herbert Orchestra in America and conducted programmes of light music. He composed forty-three operettas, including *Naughty Marietta*, *Prince Ananias* and *The Serenade*.

The music of the brass band is usually associated with all things military. The band marched the troops into battle and provided the music for the soldiers when on parade, dressed in their Number One uniforms. Patrick Sarsfield Gilmore was one such bandmaster and in his time was hailed as 'the father of the American band'. This Galway man's greatest composition was the rollicking 'When Johnny Comes Marching Home'.

The year 1951 was very important for Irish music as two organisations came into being that have since gone from strength to strength. Both have gained international renown and have been responsible for the fostering of two entirely different musical genres. Comhaltas Ceoltóirí Eireann was founded by a small committee of traditional musicians who had gathered in the town of Mullingar. It now has branches all over Ireland, England and America. The Fleadh Cheoil is the annual coming-together where musicians vie with each other in competition for All-Ireland honours. Master classes in all aspects of the music, song and dance are conducted by the very top tutors who pass on the finer points of their art.

In the same year a group of opera buffs launched the first Wexford Festival of Opera and the Arts. The group was led by a medical doctor, Dr T.J. Walsh, who had the necessary drive and courage of his convictions, that opera in October in a small seaside town in the south-east of Ireland would be a success. Balfe's *Rose of Castile* was the first opera performed in the pocket-sized Theatre Royal, followed by works in Italian, French, Russian and Czech. Many world-class singers performed in Wexford, including Mirella Freni.

On the following pages you will find the profiles of thirty Masters of Irish Music, which appeared periodically in *Ireland's Own* some time ago and which I have enjoyed researching and writing for your reading pleasure. You might just dip into and out of this book as the humour takes you or use it as a work of reference – especially when writing or preparing programme notes for a concert or a talk to your local historical or musical society. You will have noticed that all of the people profiled have passed on, leaving new generations to take up the challenge to continue the work started by these masters of Irish music. Happy reading.
Liam Gaul

Wexford, 2006

Photographs courtesy of Harry Bradshaw (John Feeney chapter)

Photographs are courtesy of Basil Walsh, Delray Beach, Florida, USA (Balfe chapter)

Photographs copyright to Basil Walsh, Delray Beach, Florida, USA (Catherine Hayes chapter)

Photographs courtesy of the Denis O'Connor Photographic Archive (For Walsh chapter)

1.

Carolan – Journeys with a Harp, a Horse, and a Helper

Born in 1670 in Spiddal in the parish of Nobber, County Meath, Turlough O'Carolan was the last of the Irish harper-composers. Over 200 of his compositions still exist. Blinded by smallpox at the age of eighteen, Carolan adopted music as a career, travelling the countryside for most of his lifetime and staying at the Big Houses where he entertained the company with his playing and singing. He frequently visited Dublin, where he was a familiar figure and often joined Italian composers such as Geminiani and Corelli. The meeting between Carolan and Geminiani took place at the behest of the Italian composer, who played a piece of music in the Italian style with a number of subtle, deliberate mistakes. Asked for his opinion, Carolan replied, 'Fine, though here and there it limps and stumbles'. He then proceeded to play the piece back, after just one hearing, correcting the mistakes by adding his own improvisation, and so *Carolan's Concerto* came into existence.

Before losing his sight, Carolan had received a good education with the children of Mrs Mary MacDermott Roe of Alderford, who had her own teacher. Carolan's father, John, worked for the MacDermott Roes, who carried on an ironworks business at Ballyfarnon. Following his blindness, Mrs MacDermott Roe sent Carolan to learn the harp with another MacDermott Roe, with whom he studied for three years – up to his twenty-first birthday. His apprenticeship complete, Mrs MacDermott Roe provided Carolan with a harp, a horse, and a helper. Money in his pocket, he set out on the roads of Ireland to earn his living as a musician.

According to Edward Bunting, Carolan was not a great performer on the harp, but extremely talented as a poet. In his introduction to *The Ancient Music of Ireland*, published in 1840, Bunting states, 'He never excelled as a performer: this may be attributed to the fact that he did not begin to learn the harp till he was upwards

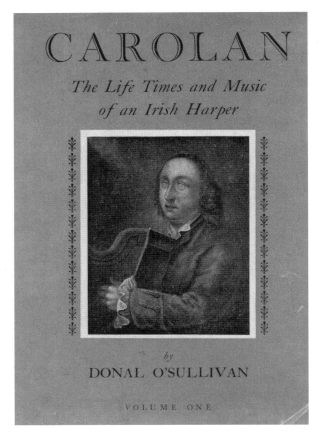

The cover of Volume One of two volumes of the life, times and music of an Irish harper by Donal O'Sullivan. They contain the compositions of Carolan.

of sixteen, at which age the fingers have lost their suppleness that must be taken advantage of in early years to produce a really master hand'. Whatever his stand-ard of playing or proficiency on his instrument, Carolan certainly was a prolific composer, leaving 170 tunes for patrons, 10 without titles, 25 miscellaneous tunes and 8 laments. A total of 213 compositions are extant and set down in musical notation. Their popularity is evident in the many recordings of his compositions by harpers, harpsichordists, flautists, recorder ensembles, and chamber groups that delight our ears. His music had a regal flavour and is still played and enjoyed today, over 200 years after Carolan's death in 1738.

Having left Alderford, Carolan's first port of call was the house of George Reynolds, Letterfian, County Leitrim, where he composed the graceful piece 'Sheebeg and Sheemore'. He was rewarded by Reynolds with a horse for his helper, who up until then had walked ahead of Carolan, who was on horseback. At the O'Farrell's residence in County Longford he composed several pieces, one of which was a jig in praise of James O'Farrell's wife, formerly Mary Nugent. Carolan's travels in Ireland covered quite a large area in the southern counties, with

The Carolan harp, from the
seventeenth or eighteenth century.

occasional trips to Ulster, where he visited Antrim, Cavan, Donegal, Fermanagh,
Monaghan, and Tyrone. On one of those trips he visited Art McCooey, the Ulster
poet and composer of the poem 'Máire Dhall' (Blind Mary). It is possible that
Carolan brought the melody for this poem down south with him, as this tune is
attributed to Carolan, but there is no proof that he was the composer.

The Maguires of Tempo were patrons of the blind bard, and the tune
'Constantine Maguire' is a reminder of those proud Ulster noblemen. Carolan
travelled Galway, Leitrim, Mayo, Roscommon and Sligo in the province of
Connaught; Dublin, Kildare, Longford, Louth, Meath and Westmeath in Leinster;
and only Clare in Munster.

Many of Carolan's compositions are in praise of the O'Connors, McDermotts,
O'Rourkes, the Nugents, the Maguires, and Lord and Lady Dillon – families that
held on to the old ways and the old faith. He also composed planxties for Squire
Jones, John Irwin, Mrs Maxwell, Mrs Cole, Lady Athenry and Lord Inchiquin of
Dromoland Castle, all of whom were either of English stock or belonged to fami-
lies who had accepted the conquest and survived to thrive once again. Carolan

belonged to a class of Irish harpers and poets who followed a tradition established centuries earlier, who visited the Big Houses for the patronage of the occupants, and in turn composed musical pieces in their honour – the origins of their patrons was of no great concern to the bards. Special occasions were marked by dedicated compositions from Carolan and an abundance of whiskey – to which Carolan was very partial – and good cheer. Other occasions included the first Christmas night that the O'Connors spent in their new house at Belanagare and the marriages of his patrons – Major Conmee to Elizabeth Nugent, John Cole to Jean Saunderson, and John Drury to Elizabeth Goldsmith. Sad times were marked by elegies that Carolan composed, such as on the deaths of Sir Ulick Burke of Glinsk, Terence MacDonough, the celebrated lawyer, and Owen O'Rourke, the hereditary Prince of Breffni.

From the titles of his compositions it is easy to see that Carolan stayed at the homes of the 'descendants of the Gael' and the homes of their supplanters alike. These sojourns resulted in the 213 melodies that survive only as single line melodies. We have no idea as to how Carolan accompanied or harmonized them, and there is only one surviving copy of an original publication by Carolan's son and Dr Delaney, which is held by the National Library of Ireland. Missing its title page, this book is thought to be a copy of the work published by Carolan's son, which places its publication date at around 1748. It is amazing to think that Turlough O'Carolan traversed no less than eighteen counties of Ireland during his forty-seven years of wanderings. The blind harper eventually returned to Mary MacDermott Roe at Alderford, where he died on 25 March 1738. Shortly before his death he composed his final tune, 'Carolan's Farewell to Music'. It was said that he had a memorable funeral, that his wake lasted four days and was attended by clergymen, gentlemen, and a vast number of country people. Within the burial ground in the old church of Kilronan is the burial place of the MacDermott Roe family and there is a stone that states:

'Within this Churchyard lies interred CAROLAN The last of the Irish Bards. He died March, 25th, 1738. R.I.P.'

2.

Edward Bunting and the Belfast Harp Festival

Edward Bunting was born in Armagh in 1773, one of three sons. His father was an English mining engineer and his mother was an O'Neill from Derry. Tragedy struck the Bunting family with the death of Edward's father in 1782, when Edward was only seven years of age. His eldest brother, Anthony, was then living and teaching music in Drogheda, County Louth, and it was to him that young Bunting was sent to study music. Anthony Bunting also gave piano lessons at 44 Mount Street, Dublin, while another brother, John, was a music teacher and music seller at 3 Donegall Street in Belfast

Edward was something of a prodigy, and at the age of eleven he was apprenticed to William Ware, organist at St Anne's Church in Belfast. Ware was deemed the 'father of music in Belfast' and was a renowned teacher of harpsichord, spinet, pianoforte and guitar. It was in answer to Ware's advertisement for an apprentice aged between nine and twelve that Bunting was taken on. The advertisement in the *Belfast Newsletter* read as follows: 'A fee is required. None need apply who cannot be well recommended and who has not a taste for the musical profession', so those were the conditions under which Bunting was accepted as an apprentice in 1784. He studied piano and organ with William Ware and was also taught the skills of reconstructing and repairing pianos. Edward lodged with the McCracken family who were deeply involved in politics. The young Bunting was soon in demand as an organist and he gave music lessons in the city, where he became a popular and successful professional musician.

It was evident by the late eighteenth century that traditional Irish harpers were scarce and the music of the harpers was nearly extinct. In the hope of halting this decline, and to encourage and preserve the old harping tradition, newspaper advertisements were placed, inviting all Irish harpers to participate in a harpers' festival to be held in Belfast in 1792. Even though prizes were offered for the three

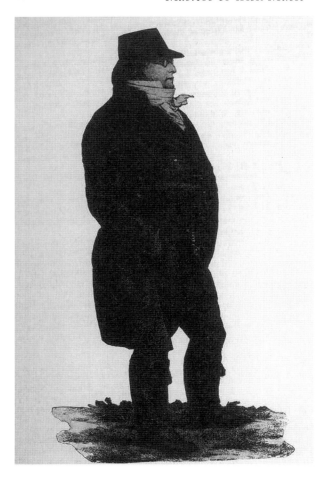

Edward Bunting, who not only noted the music of the harpers but also details of the actual playing techniques. Engraving of Edward Bunting by William Brocas, 1811.

best performers and a consolation prize for all participants, only ten Irish harpers and one Welsh harper turned up to compete. The list of competitors included the following performers: Charles Fanning, 56; Arthur O'Neill, 58; Denis Hempson, 97; Hugh Higgins, 55; Charles Byrne, 80; Daniel Black, 74; Patrick Quinn, 47; James Duncan, 45; William Carr, 15; Rose Mooney, 52 – the only female player – and a Welsh Harper named Williams, of whom little is known.

The nineteen-year-old Edward Bunting was commissioned to write down the tunes played by the harpers in music manuscript. It is thanks to his diligence in annotating not only the old harp tunes but also clues as to the method and style of playing used by the old harpers, that we have all the information that has come down to us today. He also collected lore and technical information in his notebooks over the three days of the festival, which was held from 11 to 13 July 1792. The venue was the Exchange Rooms Ballroom. Bunting moved among the harpers taking notes about the music while the citizens of Belfast came and went, having paid an admission fee of half a guinea at the door. It was attended by the nobility and gentry of the day, as well as by people like Mary Anne and Henry Joy McCracken and Theobald Wolfe Tone, who recorded some very harsh comments about the harpers in his diary.

It is clear that the most important person at the Belfast Harp Festival was Edward Bunting, and the significance of his presence is underlined by the music he collected over those three days. His interest in ancient music was to continue long after the festival ended, and he undertook several collecting tours around the countryside between 1792 and 1809. Bunting was just in time to save this music for posterity, because by 1809 all but two of the harpers who had played at Belfast were dead.

As a nation we are indebted to Edward Bunting for making the following tunes available to us today – and they form the basis of what is the very best in the repertoire of traditional performers: tunes like 'An Chúilfhionn', 'Eibhlín a Rúin', 'Táimse im Codladh', 'Róisín Dubh', 'Casadh' and 'tSugáin' and many of the Carolan melodies. The organising committee of the Belfast Harp Festival stipulated that Bunting would note the many tunes played by the harpers without any changes or alterations whatsoever. He did not adhere to this directive, however, and in his published collections many of the tunes were arranged for piano, and would not have been playable on the harp as they were. The sixty-six tunes in his first volume, published in 1796, are simple arrangements and are suitable for the Irish harp, while his 1809 publication is more elaborate. Of the seventy-seven tunes, only a few are suited to the harp, with the majority having complicated piano accompaniments that take from the character of the music. His third and final volume of one-hundred and fifty-one airs and information on harp techniques, published in 1840, is totally unplayable on the harp without considerable alteration and adaptation.

The jovial, fun-loving Edward Bunting married Marianne Chapman in 1819 and moved to Dublin, where Edward became organist as well as giving music lessons at St Stephen's Church. He visited Paris, Belgium, and Holland. It was another music collector, George Petrie, who encouraged Bunting to publish his final collection in 1840 and who said of him: 'of all the collectors, Bunting, was the only one qualified for the task, through his love of Irish music, and he alone understood its character and style and felt its peculiarities'. Soon after his final publication, Edward Bunting took ill and died suddenly on 21 December 1843. He is buried in Mount Jerome Cemetery, Dublin.

3.

Thomas Moore and
Moore's Melodies

Thomas Moore, son of John and Anastatia Moore, was born on 28 May 1779 in Dublin. So many of us are familiar with the poetry of Moore, and most of us have our favourites. 'The Minstrel Boy', 'Meeting of the Waters', 'Oft in the Stilly Night', 'The Harp that Once through Tara's Halls' or 'Let Erin Remember' are the poems most often taught in our school days for concerts, feiseanna or choral competitions, and they have stayed in our minds since. Moore's melodies are still performed 150 years after his death.

It was while a student at Trinity College that Moore first discovered the collected works of Bunting, just one year following their publication, in 1797. Moore credited Edward Bunting with having first made him aware of the 'beauties of our native music'. Thomas Moore was a very competent pianist and together with his friend Edward Hudson, a flautist, spent many hours playing the tunes collected by Edward Bunting, the young Belfast organist.

Following the successful publication of Robert Burns' adaptations of Scottish songs in Edinburgh during the 1790s, William and James Power, two Dublin music-sellers, thought they might publish a similar set of Irish songs. They approached Thomas Moore while he was visiting his native Dublin in 1806, outlining their idea. Moore immediately appreciated the possibilities of this idea and contacted John Stevenson, the Irish composer, commissioning him to make piano arrangements for his selected airs.

A total of 124 Irish airs were selected and wed to Moore's poetry between the years 1808 to 1834. His first volume of twelve songs entitled *Irish Melodies* contained eight melodies taken from the Bunting collection. Eventually, Moore used a total of twenty-six transcriptions from Edward Bunting's massive collection of rich melodic airs. In this first publication Moore included the poem 'Oh! Breathe Not His Name', which was a tribute to his friend Robert Emmet. The

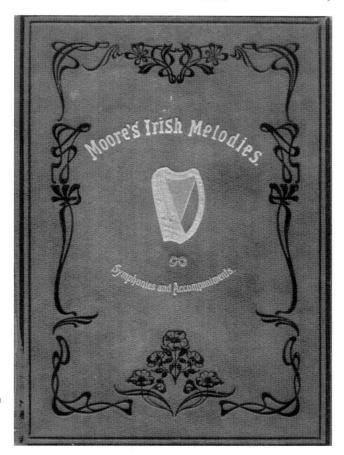

Moore's Irish Melodies – with symphonies and accompaniments by Sir John Stevenson and an introduction and preface by Dr W.H. Grattan Flood.

air he used was an O'Carolan composition in praise of Doctor John Stafford.

In the preface to Volume One, published on 1 April 1808, Moore stated: 'we have too long neglected the collection of Our National Music'. Praising the wonderful work of Edward Bunting, Moore stated that he believed that we had left these treasures of melody unclaimed, with many of our airs being used to enrich operas and sonatas of continental composers without even an acknowledgement of their origin. An instant success, with a second volume published later in the same year, Moore was offered a contract of £500 per annum for a further series, a handsome sum for the twenty-seven year-old poet. Moore, of course, had many works other than his *Irish Melodies* published. With his strong political views and with a government that maintained the right to threaten or suppress publishers and authors who expressed patriotic sentiments in poetry or prose, Moore had only one course of action – to emigrate. England, the oppressor, became a safe haven for Thomas Moore.

Moore was a short man, scarcely five feet tall, with dark, curly hair and deep-set

Portrait of Thomas Moore by Martin Shee.

eyes, with a boyish look that endeared him to everyone. He won the respect of the most influential people of the time including Sir Walter Scott, Lord John Russell, editor and poet Leigh Hunt, the publisher John Murray, Lord Landsdowne, and Lord Byron, the poet.

Moore was accused of turning his back on his native land and on the dying vestiges of Irish culture, yet his poetry and *Irish Melodies*, which otherwise might have been lost, contributed in no small way to the popularity and preservation of Irish culture. The third volume of *Irish Melodies* appeared in May 1810, with a dedication to the Dowager Marchioness of Donegal. An 'Introductory for the Pianoforte', consisting of four old airs, prefaced this publication.

The following year, 1811, saw the publication of a fourth volume, with a fifth collection following in 1813. Thomas Moore had intended to conclude the series with a sixth and final volume in 1815, but the phenomenal success of the other publications changed his mind. In 1818 and 1821 the seventh and eighth volumes were published. Sir John Stevenson was credited with the symphonies and accompaniments in the Dublin edition of 1818, while a London edition of the melodies gave the musical credit to Sir Henry Bishop. Due to differences with his Dublin publishers, the ninth edition was published in London. They were known as *Moore's Melodies* even though not even one of the melodies was composed by Moore himself. A tenth volume was published in 1834, bringing the total of songs to 124, including two of our most famous and lyrical melodies: 'An Chuilfhionn' and 'The Groves of Blarney', better known as 'The Last Rose of Summer'.

The German-born composer Friedrich von Flotow (1812–1883) was so enamoured of the melodious 'Last Rose of Summer' that he included it in his opera *Martha*. First performed in 1847, Martha sings 'Letzte Rose' to her Lyonel at the Richmond Fair. Flotow wished that he had composed this musical delight himself. Mendelssohn, Berlioz, Duparc and Benjamin Britten all made their own arrangements of Moore's songs. Numerous musical critics have castigated Thomas Moore for his mishandling of and meddling with our ancient Irish music, which he used to float his poetry. Dominic Behan expressed his contempt for Moore in a verse of his ballad 'The Sea Around Us', which states:

Tom Moore made these waters of fame and renown,
A great lover of anything dressed in a crown,
In brandy the bandy old Saxon he'd drown,
But throw ne'er a one into the ocean.

*c.*1965, Coda Music Ltd.

The criticism of Moore's poetic talent and of his selectiveness when it came to our ancient melodies must be viewed in light of all of his work that praised his native land and its heroes. He did this at the highest literary level in English society without losing his identity or his love of Ireland. Thomas Moore refused the opportunity to be named 'Irish Poet Laureate' because, he said, 'it would have meant singing the praises of the court.' By combining poetry and melody Moore really created a series of art songs with tonal nuances, rhythms and metre directly from the old Gaelic tradition, which could be compared to the *Lieder* of Schubert, Schumann and Wolf.

Moore married actress Betsy Dyke and the couple had five children, all of whom predeceased Moore. He lapsed into senile dementia in 1849, dying on 25 February 1852 in his seventy-third year. Thomas Moore is buried in the church-yard of St Nicholas' Church at Bromham in Wiltshire. He lived at Sloperton Cottage for thirty-five years. An eighteen-foot Celtic cross marks his tomb and the plinth carries Moore's own lines:

Dear Harp of my country in darkness I found thee,
The cold chain of silence had hung o'er thee long,
When proudly, my own Island Harp, I unbound thee,
And gave all thy chords to light, freedom and song.

What better way to remember poet, musician, singer, wit and writer Thomas Moore, than with these words and his legacy of poems and melodies.

4.

John Field – Composer and Musical Inventor

Most students of classical piano have studied and played a Chopin nocturne. Following the initial learning of the notes, fingering, ornamentation, dynamics, and texture of the musical notation comes the more difficult task of interpreting and expressing the piece as Chopin might have done himself. Deemed 'the poet of the piano', Chopin adopted the form and style of the nocturne from its inventor, Irishman John Field, who was both a pianist and composer. Field invented and developed this musical form in 1814 while living in Russia, of which more below.

John Field, the first son of Robert Field, of Golden Lane, Dublin, was born on 26 July 1782, and was baptised at St Werburgh's church on 30 September. His father and grandfather were professional musicians – Robert was a violinist in the orchestras of the Dublin theatres, and his father, also John, was a church organist. Following early music lessons from his family, young John showed an aptitude for the piano, so his father sent him to study with Tommaso Giordani, a noted Italian violinist who had settled in Dublin in 1779. It was Giordani who sponsored Field's first public performance at the three 'Spiritual Concerts' given at the Rotunda Assembly Rooms in 1792. Master Field, as he was listed on the programme, played a pedal harp concerto by Madame Krumpholtz at the first concert on 24 March, and played a new concerto composed by Signor Giordani at the second concert on 4 April. At the final concert in the series on 14 April, Field performed to great acclaim.

Before the Field family departed for London in 1793, two of John's compositions had already been published. Both were variations on traditional dance tunes; they were 'Logie of Buchan', and an arrangement of the dance tune 'Speed the Plough'. This was quite an achievement for one so young.

Whether it was to improve Robert Field's musical prospects or to launch his talented son's career in music, the move to London obviously benefited both father and son. Robert joined the orchestra of the Haymarket Theatre, while John began an apprenticeship with Muzio Clementi, the famous Italian pianist, composer, publisher, and entrepreneur. The term of Field's apprenticeship was seven years, for which his father paid Clementi a fee of one hundred guineas. Four months later, on December 12 1793, John Field gave his first London performance at the London Tavern. He played 'A Lesson on the New Grand Pianoforte'. This was a benefit concert under the patronage of the Prince of Wales.

John Field's tutor went into business with several partners, including Collard, the piano maker, in the manufacture and sale of pianos. Clementi kept his brilliant student for several years and got him to play on his pianos in order to help sell them.

In 1801, Field played his own concerto at an Oratorio Concert at Covent Garden and was rewarded with wild applause – this brought him into the public arena once again. Clementi was also in the music publishing business, and he published Field's three sonatas in A, E flat, and C minor, all of which were dedicated to his master Clementi. August 1802 saw Field and Clementi set off for Paris where Field's performances of Bach, Handel and Clementi took Paris by storm. He was met with similarly positive responses in Vienna and Innsbruck.

At the close of that year both pianists arrived in St Petersburg, where Clementi opened a piano showroom – business once again being uppermost in his mind. The neglected apprentice, now twenty years of age, was dressed in ill-fitting clothes, had little money in his pocket, and was still demonstrating pianos for the greedy Clementi.

Following Clementi's departure from St Petersburg, Field found a patron in General Markloffsky, and soon found himself a large and aristocratic clientele. He was in great demand for concerts and recitals all over the city; his star was in the ascent and he played concerts as a virtuoso and became a teacher of renown. Field was at last making money from his talents, and he became fluent in French, German and Russian. In 1808 he married young French actress Adelaide Percheron, who had been one of his pupils and by whom he had a son.

In the late summer of 1814 John Field's first three nocturnes, a sonata, and his 'Rondo Ecossais' ('Speed the Plough') were published by Breitkopf & Hartels of Leipzig. Field had quite a lot of his compositions published by them and by Dalmas of St Petersburg during his lifetime. The list of his works is quite impressive and varied, including sixteen nocturnes and seven other descriptive pieces for solo piano, as well as seven concertos for piano and orchestra as well as his 'Fantasie sur un air russe', a serenade, four string quartets, and a piano and string quintet. As well as this he composed four sonatas, three of which were composed in London, and his catalogue also includes four fantasias, five rondos, eight études, five piano duets, six variations, one *marche triomphale* (composed in 1812 following the defeat of Napoleon in Russia) and two songs. Field obviously was a very prolific composer as well as performer.

Muzio Clementi (1752–1832), who was a child prodigy as an organist and composer. He went into the business of making pianos as a partner in the firm of Clementi & Co., later Collard and Collard.

Among John Field's pupils were Glinka and Mayer, both of whom regarded their master as a virtuoso and wonderful teacher. In 1822 Field settled in Moscow for a time, where he earned large sums of money through his concerts and teaching connections. Returning to London in 1832 to play a concert at the invitation of the Philharmonic Society, Field was given a warm reception by an admiring and appreciative audience. He also played at the Haydn Centenary and had the pleasure of meeting Mendelssohn. Sadly, Muzio Clementi, his old master, died on 10 March and was accorded a public funeral at Westminster Abbey, where John Field was one of the chief mourners.

Field's reception in Paris, Brussels, Toulouse, Marseilles, and Lyons was even warmer and more enthusiastic than in London. While in Naples in 1834, Field became seriously ill with cancer and was hospitalised for nine months following surgery. The noble Russian Rachmanoff family came to his aid and eventually brought Field back to Russia with them. He gave his last professional concert in Vienna, at the request of Carl Czerny. Early in 1837, his health declined further and he passed away on 11 January. He was buried on 15 January in Wedensky Kirchkof, Moscow.

Field was the inventor of a style of piano-playing that differed markedly from the existing virtuoso mode. For anyone interested in listening to some of his music, Veronica McSwiney has recorded the 'Field Nocturnes' on a two-CD set, while John O'Connor has recorded the complete piano concertos with the Irish Chamber Orchestra on a three-CD set for Claddagh Records, giving us the opportunity to enjoy the music of one of Ireland's greatest composers in exile, John Field.

5.

Julius Benedict and the Irish Operatic Ring

The Irish Ring comprises three operas: *The Lily of Killarney*, *The Bohemian Girl*, and *Maritana*. Two of the operas were composed by Irish composers Balfe and Wallace, and their storylines are set outside of Ireland, while *The Lily of Killarney* is set in Killarney, County Kerry. Just as Wagner's famous *Ring of the Nibelungen* consisted of a cycle of four operas, the *Irish Ring* consisted of the three above-mentioned works, which were to be performed on consecutive nights with full orchestral accompaniment. *The Lily of Killarney* is often associated with *The Colleen Bawn*, by Dion Boucicault (*c.*1882 – 1890) and Julius Benedict. Even though these two very talented gentlemen had what may have sounded like odd surnames to Irish ears, Boucicault was an Irishman, and although Benedict was German-born, we seem to regard and claim him as one of our own.

Julius Benedict was born in Stuttgart, Germany, on 27 November 1804, the son of a Jewish banker. His musical talent soon came to the fore, and the young Benedict was fortunate enough to learn musical composition from Johann Nepomuk Hummel at Weimar, and Carl Maria Weber at Dresden. Weber treated Benedict like a son during the three very happy years that he spent under his tutelage. It was in Vienna that Weber introduced the young Benedict to Beethoven on 15 October 1823. Following appointments as *Kappellmeister* in Vienna and Naples, Benedict went on to Paris and then, in 1835, London – at the suggestion of Maria Malibran, the Spanish soprano. Julius Benedict lived at No.2 Manchester Square for the remainder of his life.

Benedict spent a lot of his time conducting both opera and concerts, and was principal conductor of the Norwich Festival from 1845 to 1878, and the Liverpool Philharmonic Society from 1876 to 1880. He had established himself as one of England's foremost orchestral conductors, and was rated as a superb concert pianist and accompanist. It was in the capacity of piano accompanist

A portrait of the
young Julius Benedict,
who was born on 27
November 1804.

that Julius Benedict travelled to America in 1850, at the request of Jenny Lind
– the Swedish Nightingale. The concert tour was promoted by none other than
Phineas T. Barnum, famous impresario and circus owner. It is interesting to note
that Benedict's fee, including travel from London to America, plus all hotel and
travelling expenses for the 150 concerts through America, was £5,000 – with
half of this figure to be paid in advance. Benedict had conducted Mendelssohn's
Elijah at Exeter Hall, and this was the first appearance by Jenny Lind in
oratorio.

   To crown his musical career, Sir Julius Benedict was conferred with a knighthood for his contribution to music in England. He composed many operatic
works, among them *Giacinta ed Ernesto* in 1827, *I Portoghesi in Goa* in 1830, *Un
anno ed un giorno* in 1836, *The Gypsy's Warning* in 1838, *The Brides of Venice* in 1844,
The Crusaders in 1846, and *The Bride of Song* in 1864. His cantatas included *Undine*,
written in1860, *Richard Coeur de Lion*, 1863; *Graziella*, 1882; and among his oratorios were *St Cecilia*, 1886; and *St Peter*, 1870. He also composed two symphonies,
two piano concertos and, of course, *The Lily of Killarney*, which premiered at
Covent Garden, London on 8 February 1862. The libretto was by John Oxenford
and Dion Boucicault and was based on the play *The Colleen Bawn* by Boucicault,
1859. *The Lily of Killarney* proved to be a very popular opera and was always in the

Sir Julius Benedict in later life. He received a knighthood for his contribution to music.

repertoire of opera companies visiting Ireland, such as The Carl Rosa; Moody-Manners, and Bowyer and Westwood.

The main characters in the piece are the impecunious gentleman Hardress Cregan, his loyal manservant Danny Mann, Eily O'Connor – who is known as the Colleen Bawn or the Lily of Killarney and is the local beauty, Myles-na-Coppaleen, the wealthy Mistress Ann Chute, and the clergyman Father Tom. The action is set in Killarney, and the entire story hinges on Cregan, who is secretly married to seventeen-year-old Eily O'Connor. Cregan's estate is heavily mort-gaged, and the mortgage holder is the scheming landlord Corrigan. Corrigan insists that Hardress romance the wealthy mistress so that she will pay Cregan's debts to Corrigan once she and Cregan are married. Danny Mann, Cregan's serv-ant, tries to retrieve Eily O'Connor's marriage certificate so that Hardress can marry Ann Chute, but does not succeed. In his fury at her refusal to return it, Danny throws Eily overboard from a boat. Myles sees what happens from the lakeside, shoots at the figure in the boat, and mortally wounds Danny. He then rescues Eily, revives her, and hides her in the woods. Danny confesses on his death-bed to killing the Colleen Bawn, and Cregan is arrested for setting up his wife's murder, just as he is about to marry Ann Chute. Eily O'Connor arrives on the scene, declares that she is Cregan's true and lawful wife, and as there is no murder, all ends well with Mistress Chute redeeming the mortgage and returning the estate to Cregan and Eily.

Like many operas of that period, this one contains a lot of spoken dialogue interspersed with solo arias, duets, trios, and choruses, and is accompanied by a full orchestra. The *Lily of Killarney* has a wonderfully melodic male duet between tenor and baritone – 'The Moon Had Raised her Lamp Above', made famous by the John McCormack and Reinald Werenratt recording. Other highlights include 'I'm Alone, I'm Alone' which is sung by Eily O'Connor, and the poignant 'Eily Mavoureen', sung by the hero, Hardress Cregan. Danny Mann has an aria with lyrics that sound something like this: 'The Colleen Bawn, the Colleen Bawn, from childhood I have loved you', and he goes on to declare, in a loud, threatening voice, 'Shall I this gem destroy? Shall I this gem destroy?'

It is a pity that this opera, and the music of Julius Benedict, are not performed in Ireland on a more regular basis, because they are beautiful pieces of music.

6.

Michael William Balfe and *The Bohemian Girl*

The Bohemian Girl by Michael William Balfe is the third and final opera of *The Irish Ring*. Like the other two works, *Maritana* and *The Lily of Killarney*, Balfe's opera is rarely performed these days – and more is the pity. Arias such as 'The Fair Land of Poland', 'The Heart Bowed Down', 'Then You'll Remember Me' and the opera's most popular aria, 'I Dreamt that I Dwelt in Marble Halls' are just some of the musical delights from this opera.

The story is set in the Austrian city of Presburg in the late eighteenth century, with the main plot revolving around a young nobleman officer, Thaddeus of Poland, and his love for Count Arnheim's young daughter, Arline. Following many episodes of mistaken identity, the young Arline's kidnap by a band of gypsies (with whom she lives for twelve years), the jealous love of the Gipsy Queen for the handsome Thaddeus (which eventually results in the death of the Queen), and Thaddeus revealing his true identity, all ends well. Count Arnheim gives his daughter's hand in marriage to the Polish nobleman, peace is restored, and the feud between Austria and Poland is resolved. Arline is restored to her rightful place and all ends in happiness.

The composer, Michael William Balfe, was born on 15 May 1808 at No. 10 Pitt Street, now Balfe Street, which is off present-day Grattan and Grand Canal Streets in Dublin. The Balfe family was a musical one, with the young Balfe's grandfather playing in the band of a Dublin theatre while Michael's father, a dancing-master, was also a very good violinist. It was from his father that Balfe received his first music lessons. Michael went on to be tutored by William O'Rourke, who arranged for the seven-year-old 'Master Balfe' to play a concerto at a Dublin concert to great acclaim in May 1817. Balfe, a child prodigy who not only performed but was also a budding composer, had several of his ballad compositions included in the repertoire of many notable singers of the time. In 1823 Balfe's father died,

The statue of Michael William Balfe at the Theatre Royal, Drury Lane, London.

and the young musician decided to make the move to London in the hope of furthering his professional career.

In the bustling metropolis, Balfe studied with Charles Edward Horn as an articled pupil contracted for a period of seven years. Very soon an unsuccessful debut at the Oratorio Concerts proved to Balfe that further study and training were necessary, so he studied diligently over the next few years. He also had to earn a living to survive, so he played violin at Drury Lane Theatre and used his reasonable baritone voice as a means of generating additional income. The role of Caspar in *Der Freischütz* was not appreciated by Norwich audiences, but all was not lost. Balfe met Count Mazzara in London, who offered to take him to Italy for musical and vocal training, for which the count was willing to bear all expenses. Balfe lived in Rome with the Count and his family for some time before moving on to Milan.

Here he studied singing and composition, including music for a ballet which enjoyed considerable and remarkable success and played to great acclaim. He soon moved to Paris where he encountered Cherubini, the ageing and very stern master composer who introduced Balfe to Gioacchino Rossini. Having listened to Balfe sing, Rossini was so impressed with the young Irishman's vocal potential

A noted operatic singer, Balfe sang leading roles in France and Italy. He died aged sixty-two in England on 20 October 1870.

that through a friend of Cherubini's, who provided the much-needed finances, Balfe went on to study for a year with Master Bordogni. Following a very successful debut, Balfe was contracted by the Théâtre des Italiens for the next three years at an overall fee of 60,000 francs. However, due to poor health he did not fulfil his contract and returned to the warmer climes of Italy, where he sang at Palermo and met his future wife, Hungarian-born singer Lina Roser.

A meeting with Maria Malibran, famous mezzo-soprano, helped Balfe to obtain roles in Rossini's *Othello* at La Scala in Milan, and in Venice. By this time, Balfe's skills as a composer were coming to the fore and on his return to London in 1835 he completed his first opera for London, *The Siege of Rochelle*, which premiered at the Theatre Royal, Drury Lane, on 27 October 1835. Balfe was twenty-seven years old and on the verge of a fulfilling and prolific career as a composer of opera, which yielded over thirty operas in Italian, French and English. During this time Balfe continued to sing professionally in opera and, on his first return to Dublin in 1838, he sang arias from his operas to guests at a dinner in his honour at Morrison's Hotel, Dawson Street. He gave numerous concerts and operatic performances on that visit to his home city.

A playbill for a performance of Balfe's *The Bohemian Girl* at the Theatre Royal, Drury
Lane on 7 December 1843.

Following an unsuccessful managerial post in London resulting in bankruptcy,
Balfe left for Paris where he later received a commission to write a new opera
for the opéra comique. Following this, Balfe returned to London, where his
most famous opera, *The Bohemian Girl,* was first performed at the Theatre Royal,
Drury Lane, on 27 November 1843. During this time he lived at 19 Piccadilly,
Central London, where it is most likely that he composed the bulk of this opera.
After a highly successful run of over 100 nights at Drury Lane, *The Bohemian Girl*
was presented in New York, Dublin and Philadelphia in 1844, Madrid in 1845,
Vienna and Sydney in 1846, Prague in 1847, Stockholm in 1849, Berlin in 1850,
Trieste, Brescia, Verona and Bologna in 1854, and many more cities throughout
the world.

Michael William Balfe died at his home in Rowney Abbey, Hertfordshire,
England on 20 October 1870, aged sixty-two. He had suffered with bronchial
asthma all his life and it was later complicated by pneumonia. He is buried at
Kensal Green Cemetery, London. Two of Balfe's operas were performed at the
Wexford Opera Festival when the founder-director, Dr T.J. Walsh launched this
internationally famous festival with *The Rose of Castile* in 1951 and *The Siege of
Rochelle* in 1963, which was a tribute to the composer, who lived in Wexford as a
young boy.

Of days that have as happy been,
And you'll remember me,
And you'll remember, you'll remember me

I hope these words from *The Bohemian Girl* will prompt all lovers of opera and good melodic airs to remember Michael William Balfe on the bicentenary of his birth in 2008.

7.

William Vincent Wallace – 'In Happy Moments Day by Day'

Some thoughts none other can replace,
Remembrance will recall,
Which in the flight of years we trace,
Is dearer than them all.

The above words are taken from Don José's ballad to the Queen of Spain in Wallace's opera *Maritana*. This particular opera seemed 'dearer than them all' when it came to popularity with audiences. Snatches of melody were hummed, sung or whistled by cloth-capped messenger boys as they went about their business following performances. Other numbers, such as 'Scenes that are Brightest', 'In Happy Moments', and 'Hear Me Gentle Maritana' were sung in many a drawing-room musical soirée with 'Yes! Let Me Like a Soldier Fall' and 'There is a Flower that Bloometh' being sung by the local tenor. *Maritana* premiered at Drury Lane Theatre, London, on 15 November 1845 and was part of the operatic repertoire until the Great War. *Maritana* is one of the operas that make up *The Irish Ring*. It surfaces periodically with amateur companies and light opera societies, with its vibrancy and easy-to-remember melodies.

'Tis the mem'ry of the past! It wafteth perfume o'er us, Which few can e'er forget, Of the bright scenes gone before us, Of sweet, tho' sad regret!'

William Vincent Wallace was born on 11 March 1812 in Colbeck Street, Waterford. Stationed in Waterford, his father was band-master of the 29th Worcestershire Regiment. His mother Elizabeth was a Waterford woman. Wallace had a younger brother, born in 1813, and a sister, Eliza, born in 1814. Young William displayed a remarkable musical talent and with early tuition from his

Waterford-born Michael
Vincent Wallace, who
composed the operas
Maritana, *Lurline*, and *The
Amber Witch*.

father went on to study with Otto Hamilton and John Ringwood – who was
organist at Waterford Cathedral and St Olave's Church. Aged seven, the youth
played clarinet with his father's band, eventually conducting the band at the age
of twelve. He became proficient in clarinet, piano, organ and violin and at the
age of fifteen became director of the Philharmonic Society in Dublin and played
in the orchestra in the Theatre Royal. In 1830 he was appointed as organist in
Thurles, and converted to Catholicism on his marriage to Isabella Kelly, taking
the name Vincent in honour of his new sister-in-law, a nun in Thurles.

The family settled in Dublin until 1835 when they emigrated to Australia. Five
years later Wallace deserted his wife and children, going on to spend time in
sheep-farming and whale-hunting. On a trip to India he was mauled by a tiger.
Wallace travelled extensively from the Antipodes to South America, and even
served as Director of Music at the Italian Theatre in Mexico from 1841 to 1842.

He later returned to Europe and eventually England, where he immersed himself in composing music for an opera. The main musical themes had been in
his mind since his time in Australia and the time had come to commit them to

A bust of William Vincent
Wallace at the Theatre
Royal, Waterford.

manuscript. It was in London that Wallace met a former Dublin friend, Hayward
St Leger, who introduced him to Edward Fitzball, the dramatist who provided
Wallace with the libretto of *Maritana*. The lyrics of two of the pieces from the
opera – 'Scenes that are Brightest' and 'In Happy Moments' – were written by
Alfred Bunn. The story is based on d'Ennery and Dumanoir's play *Don Caesar
de Bazan*. Following its very successful run in London, Wallace visited Dublin
to give a concert in the Rotunda on 9 February 1846. *Maritana* was produced in
Dublin later that year.

It is a complicated story of intrigue between the King and Queen of Spain, Don
José, a courtier, a way-ward Don Caesar, a gypsy girl named Maritana, Lazarillo
(a young man with a secret marriage), and it also includes a failed execution and
the eventual recognition of the true lovers, as well as the death of Don José. There
is a plot, a counter-plot, intrigue, bravado from the hero, and the entire story
comes together in a happy ending. The texts are not great but the tunes are very
melodic and contribute in no small way to the success of *Maritana*. Arias such
as 'Tis the Harp in the Air', 'Alas, Those Chimes', 'Yes!, Let Me Like a Soldier
Fall', 'In Happy Moments Day by Day', 'There Is a Flower That Bloometh', and
'Scenes that are Brightest' are all worthy musical pieces that have been sung in

many a concert and that are warmly received by audiences. *Maritana* also features very good choral work, especially the 'Angelus Chorus', Health to the Lady', and 'With Rapture Glowing'.

William Vincent Wallace composed ten operas, six of which were published: *Maritana*, 1845; *Matilda of Hungary*, 1847; *Lurline*, 1860; *The Amber Witch*, 1861; *Love's Triumph*, 1862; and *Desert Flower*, 1863. In the middle of his success with *Maritana* disaster struck: Wallace was threatened with blindness and on the advice of his doctor returned to South America for treatment, which was successful. Soon after this he moved to New York, becoming an American citizen in 1850. It was there that he bigamously married twenty-three year-old concert pianist Helene Stoepel. He claimed that his first marriage to Isabella was illegal due to the fact that he had been under twenty and a Protestant when it took place.

Wallace's health began to suffer again and from 1854 until his death he suffered a series of heart attacks. In 1864, on medical advice, he set out for a holiday in the south of France. On the journey he took ill and stayed in Paris for a while, where he had visits from such famous musicians as Giacomo Rossini, Sigismond Thalberg and George Osborne, the Limerick-born pianist-composer. Wallace died at the Chateau of Bayern in the Haute-Garonne on 12 October 1865, aged fifty-three.

8.

Catherine Hayes – The Limerick Nightingale

Ireland has some very fine female operatic singers today, but Catherine Hayes seems to have had that rare quality that placed her in the upper echelons of the operatic world. She lived, unfortunately, before the age of recording, so that we only have the reports of the journals of the day proclaiming her brilliance. A couple of very good books have also been written about her career over the years. Catherine Hayes was born at 4 Patrick Street, Limerick, on 25 October, 1818. Differing accounts put her birth date at 1825, which has caused some confusion. Her father, Arthur William Hayes, was a bandmaster attached to the local militia, and her mother, Mary Carroll, was a servant working in the household of the Earl of Limerick. Her parents married in St Michael's Church, Limerick, in 1815, and Catherine was baptised into the Protestant faith in the same church; the family belonged to the Church of Ireland. Catherine had a sister, Henrietta, and two brothers, Charles and William, both of whom died in infancy. Her father lost his job as bandmaster, and as he was a civilian there was no chance of moving with the military to another town. He abandoned his wife and family in 1825, and it is thought that he went to America or Canada. He never made contact with his wife or young daughters again, even when Catherine, at the height of her career, was touring America and Canada.

The family lived in dire poverty and the mother tried to rear her two children on her own. Mary Hayes kept her servant job with the Earl of Limerick and the meagre wage she received was her only source of income. Catherine and Henrietta received no formal education – they lived in hardship. Catherine had a nice singing voice and one day was overheard singing in the garden of the earl by Reverend Edmund Knox, the Anglican bishop who lived next to the earl's estate. He recognised Catherine's potential and very soon had her singing for influential guests at his residence. A fund was set up by the bishop's wife, Agnes,

Operatic singer Catherine Hayes, born in Limerick on 25 October 1818.

to finance musical training for Catherine. In 1839 she was sent to Dublin to study with Antonio Sapio, with great success. Concerts and recitals in Dublin and the major Irish cities enabled her to go to Paris in 1842 for further study with Manuel García, and later to Milan where her teacher was Felice Ronconi. Catherine performed in several operatic roles but excelled in *Lucia di Lammermoor*, and as Linda in Donizetti's opera *Linda di Chamounix* – after her first appearance at La Scala in Milan in 1845 she received an ovation. After a successful tour of Italy she went to England in 1849, where she was engaged for Covent Garden at a salary of £1,300 – a considerable amount of money at the time.

Catherine's most popular roles were in *Lucia di Lammermoor* and in Donizetti's *Linda di Chamounix*.

She never forgot her humble beginnings and looked after all of her mother and sister's needs, and they were the beneficiaries of her will following her early death. Catherine's mother always travelled with her on all of her tours abroad, and her success as an operatic diva took her to Venice, Florence, Genoa, Rome, and other cities in Italy, where she became the most sought-after Lucia di Lammermoor. While at Covent Garden, Catherine received an invitation to sing for Queen Victoria at Buckingham Palace in June 1849. After an evening of Italian operatic arias the Queen requested an encore and Catherine duly obliged with an Irish song – 'Kathleen Mavoureen'. Returning to Ireland during the Great Famine, she gave concerts in her native Limerick, Dublin, and Cork, garnering rave reviews from the musical critics of the day. Catherine's success was wonderful; she was met with the highest acclaim wherever she sang, and yet she maintained a shy, gentle and ladylike disposition, never forgetting her origins.

She travelled to America in 1851, when the Swedish Nightingale, Jenny Lind, was causing much excitement. Concerts in New York, Boston, Toronto,

Catherine Hayes
died suddenly at
the early age of
forty-three on 1
August 1861.

Philadelphia, and Washington DC were very successful for Catherine. She toured
the southern states, giving concerts in Charleston, Savannah, and New Orleans.
She met all the prominent people – from the President to statesmen and business people. Catherine also met her future husband, William Avery Bushnell, an
electioneering agent who had once been Jenny Lind's manager, in New York. He
became Catherine's manager for her American tour – some Americans were so
enthusiastic to see and hear the Irish prima donna that one ticket for one of her
concerts in California changed hands for $1,000. Catherine's travels took her to
San Francisco during the gold rush, and she there sang for the miners and the
élite of that city. Her tour was sponsored by the great showman P.T. Barnum.

Catherine Hayes travelled the world singing in opera and giving performances
from Peru to Chile, Hawaii to Australia – she was the first great operatic star
from Europe to visit Australia. During her stay in Calcutta she performed for the
British military before moving on to Singapore and Java, and then returning to
Australia for further performances. Her mother travelled with her on all of those

tours before Catherine returned to England in 1856 to marry William Bushnell in London the following year. Tragedy struck when her husband fell into poor health and died in Biarritz on 2 July 1858, aged just thirty-five. Catherine continued to perform in London with recitals of drawing-room ballads that proved very popular.

After her difficult childhood and youth, Catherine Hayes had reached the pinnacle of her profession and was the toast of the operatic world in many cities, delighting her audiences. Her death from a stroke at the age of forty-three was sudden and unexpected, and occurred at her friend Henry Lee's home at Sydenham, Kent, on 1 August, 1861. She is buried at Kensal Green Cemetery, London. Known as the Limerick Nightingale, Catherine Hayes' life was a classical rags to riches story.

9

Patrick Sarsfield Gilmore 'When Johnny Comes Marching Home'

Regarded as 'the Father of the American Navy', Commodore John Barry has a counterpart in Patrick Sarsfield Gilmore, who is regarded as 'the Father of the American Band'. Who was Gilmore and what role did he play in the musical history of the 'New World'? Many of us are familiar with John Philip Sousa who was famous for his wonderful, soul-stirring military marches like 'Stars and Stripes Forever', 'The Washington Post', and 'El Capitan', but it was P.S. Gilmore who was responsible for the foundation of American Marching Bands prior to the young Sousa gaining much of the credit.

Born on Christmas Day 1829 in Ballygar, County Galway, Patrick Steven Gilmore (he would change the middle section of his name in later life) was the son of a stone-cutter. His parents hoped he would enter the priesthood but the young Gilmore was more interested in musical matters, playing the fife in the local band. As a member of the Ballygar Fife and Drum Band, Patrick paraded at a monster protest rally in Athlone with his father, who was also a band member. As a garrison town, Athlone had several British Army bands that paraded at that gathering, much to young Gilmore's delight and interest. Here was the first occasion on which he witnessed modern, well-equipped and disciplined marching bands. He was smitten. He was only interested in returning to Athlone to join a good band, which he did. He was fortunate to be able to join a local band who boasted a renowned bandmaster named Patrick Keating. Keating took an interest in Gilmore, teaching him the finer points of trumpet-playing and introducing him to classical music.

With a good grounding in music and a burning ambition to succeed, P.S. Gilmore set off on an immigrant ship to Boston in 1848, where he joined a local band. After a short time Gilmore was appointed leader of the Boston Brigade Band. He then went on to play with the Charlestown Band, where his fame as a

Bandmaster and composer
Patrick Sarsfield Gilmore.

trumpeter brought offers to lead the trumpet section in many other bands. The
foremost band in America at the time was the Salem Brigade Band. Salem also
boasted a radical political party called the 'Know-Nothing Party' which despised
the Irish, Catholics and foreigners. As Gilmore qualified on all three counts he
wasn't exactly a big favourite in Salem. It was suggested that a name change
might help him to gain more musical engagements, so he changed his middle
name, Stephen, to that of one of Ireland's proudest patriotic heroes, Sarsfield.
A totally unexpected change, this didn't endear Patrick Sarsfield Gilmore to his
opponents. His musical talent could not be overlooked though, and it saw him
through.

   With the onset of the Civil War, Gilmore and the band were very much in
demand, playing at rallies and other recruiting functions. They also played for the
inauguration of President James Buchanan, fifteenth president of America.

   In 1858 P.S. Gilmore married Ellen O'Neill, and the following year returned to
Boston. On 9 April the re-organized Boston Brigade Band gave its first concert
as Patrick Gilmore's Band. On foot of a general order issued on 31 July 1861,
military bands were allowed to serve in the Union Army. Gilmore's Band enlisted,
attaching itself to the 24th Massachusetts Infantry. As well as providing music for

Gilmore in full
uniform with his
decorative medals.

the regiment, band members also served as stretcher bearers at battles in Roanoke, New Bern, Bull Run, Antietam, Fredericksburg, Chancellors Ville, Gettysburg, Chickamauga, Nashville, Petersburg, and Richmond. P.S. Gilmore composed several songs during the years of strife including 'Good News from Home', 'God Save the Nation', and 'After the Battle of Gettysburg'. Having listened to a soldier sing 'John Brown's Body' he transcribed the melody which was to become one of the greatest march songs of the war. Later, with a new set of lyrics by Julia Ward Home, it became the 'Battle Hymn of the Republic'. Undoubtedly, Gilmore's greatest composition has to be the rollicking 'When Johnny Comes Marching Home'. The lyrics are credited to Louis Lambert – which turned out to be the pen-name of Gilmore.

After the Civil War ended the Union Congress decided to deactivate Regular Army Bands due to the very high costs of rebuilding the country, and turned to using civilian bands for official and ceremonial occasions. As civilian bands were not regulated by the army, bandleaders reduced the sizes of their bands and added woodwind instruments to complement the brass sections.

Gilmore was in Paris for the 1869 International Exhibition and was greatly impressed by the pleasant blends and subtle musical colourings that the addition and combination of brass and reed instruments achieved. On his return to America he accepted the leadership of the 22nd Regiment Band of New York, and within four months the 65-man band gave its first concert, introducing America to this combination of instrumentation. The addition of saxophones, bass clarinets and Bb tubas to the band enabled them to play styles of music heretofore restricted to orchestras. Gilmore's 22nd Regiment Band now included symphonic and operatic transcriptions with the old reliable waltzes and marches in his concert programmes.

To generate goodwill throughout America following the years of Civil War, Abraham Lincoln personally requested P.S. Gilmore to organize and perform a large Peace Celebration in New Orleans. With this directive from the Commander-in-Chief, Gilmore took the opportunity to gather 500 musicians and 5,000 school children from across both Confederate and Union communities to sing patriotic songs, with the beat marked by the roar of a cannon gun. Following the New Orleans experiment, Gilmore was inspired to organize a huge Peace Festival at Cooley Square, Boston, involving 1,000 musicians and 10,000 singers. This very successful event was attended by President Grant and his cabinet. A tour of Europe by the Gilmore Band gave Gilmore the idea to stage a World Peace Jubilee on his return to America. This he did in 1872, but it proved to be a financial disaster. Despite its financial failure the World Peace Jubilee made P.S. Gilmore a national musical figure.

Gilmore created 'Gilmore's Concert Garden', later to become the first Madison Square Garden in New York. He was musical director for many important celebrations, including the 4 July Centennial in Philadelphia in 1876, and the dedication of the Statue of Liberty in 1886. His band made some of the first commercial recordings for Thomas Edison in 1891 and it was Gilmore and his band who started the tradition of greeting the new year in Times Square, New York. Patrick Sarsfield Gilmore died in 1892 and is buried with his wife and daughter in Old Calvary Cemetery, Long Island, New York. The P.S. Gilmore Society was founded in Boston in 1968 by Michael Cummings, himself a native son of Ballygar, County Galway. Mike has kept the name of P.S. Gilmore alive with many events, band competitions, scholarships, and workshops dedicated to 'the Father of the American Band'.

The laurel wreath is ready now,
To place upon his loyal brow,
When Gilmore Comes Marching Home.

10.

Johnny Patterson – The Rambler from Clare

Johnny Patterson was billed in John Swallow's circus as 'The Irish Singing Clown', and he travelled the length and breadth of Ireland, England, and the United States of America, playing to thousands in 'fit-up' shows. Patterson was born in Kilbarron, County Clare, in 1840 – just before Ireland went through the trials and hardships of the Great Famine. His father, Francis Patterson, was a nail-gunsmith or blacksmith and came from Northern Ireland. There were four children, two boys and two girls. Their mother died following the birth of the youngest child, Frank, who was fostered by an O'Hanlon family in Feakle as their father had also passed away. The two girls were raised by relatives in Killaloe, while three-year-old Johnny was sent to Ennis to live with his Uncle Mark in Mill Street. Later Johnny was apprenticed to his uncle, who was also a nailer. His great love of music was encouraged by his uncle, who enrolled the fourteen-year-old Johnny in the army as a drummer boy with the 63rd Foot Infantry based in Limerick. There he learned to play various instruments and became a competent player on the piccolo and drums

When John Swallow's circus visited Limerick, Johnny got a part-time job in the circus band. He was nineteen years old at this point, and having spent over five years in the regiment, he bought himself out of the army for £20. Johnny took off with the circus when they left Limerick, and while in Cork Johnny appeared in the ring as a solo performer, telling jokes and singing his own songs. He was such a success that he won a two-year contract with the circus and was billed as 'The Irish Singing Clown'. He disregarded the traditional circus clown's white face and pantaloons in favour of a tweed outfit decorated with shamrocks and an Irish harp, and wore white knee-length stockings and a cone-shaped hat, as well as a large drooping handlebar moustache that completed this 'new look' Irish clown.

His different costume and different style of clowning, together with his Irish songs and wit, made Johnny Patterson a popular entertainer in the circus ring. He was a fluent Irish speaker and an excellent uilleann piper, and his signature song was 'I Am a Roving Irish Boy'. Patterson never lost his sense of humour and readiness to laugh, despite the devastating effects of the famine and mass emigration. Many of his early song compositions have been lost, but many other later songs are still popular today, among them 'The Stone Outside Dan Murphy's Door', 'The Garden Where the Praties Grow', 'Good-bye Johnny Dear', 'Shake hands with Your Uncle Dan', 'The Old Turf Fire', 'Bridget Donohue', and 'I'll Remember You Love In My Prayers'.

When the Swallow Circus left Ireland, Patterson found work first with Batty's and then Risarelli's Circus. On a visit to Liverpool with the Pablo Franque Circus in 1869 he met James and Selena Hickey, a brother and sister bareback-riding partnership from Scotland. By the end of the season, Johnny and Selena had fallen in love and were soon married in Liverpool. In 1870 their daughter Bridget was born, and a second daughter, Nora, was born in 1872. In 1875, after the family returned to Ireland, Johnny went on tour with the Powell and Clarke Circus and while away learned that his wife, who was based in Belfast, had given birth to a son, Johnny junior.

At the age of thirty-five, Johnny Patterson was a national success and could hold an audience captive with his act. Accepting an invitation from American circus Cooper and Bailey's, Patterson left for America in 1876, leaving his three children in the care of their Aunt Betty in Killaloe while Selena pursued her own circus career. Johnny became one of the most famous and highly paid performers of his time, and compositions like 'The Stone Outside Dan Murphy's Door' and 'Off to Philadelphia in the Morning' were favourites with his audiences.

'The Rambler from Clare' eventually became Johnny Patterson's signature tune, although he did not compose it himself. While in America he received the news that his daughter Nora had been killed by an elephant in her mother's circus. Johnny stayed in America, but turned to alcohol to dull the pain of his loss – and he so far away from home. He began to feel the strain of the pace of life in America, and at the age of forty-five decided to return to Ireland.

A wealthy man, he bought a house in Belfast, where he was reunited with his wife and family. He joined Lloyd's Mexican Circus and had high hopes of putting a circus of his own on the road.

In June 1886, Selena died of consumption in Belfast, resulting in their two surviving children being sent to Johnny's sister's home in Killaloe. In 1887 he joined up with Australian Joe Keeley, following which the Keeley and Patterson Circus toured Ireland. In April 1888, Johnny Patterson married Bridget Murray at Castlepollard, County Westmeath.

The political situation in Ireland around that time was worrying him, and being a Parnellite, Patterson composed a song called 'Do Your Best for One Another'.

Guerins – reputedly Dan Murphy's shop in Ennis, Co. Clare.

He performed this number wearing two small flags: a green flag with a harp and a red flag with a crown, as a symbol of the two islands working together, and of a union of harp and crown.

Johnny decided to sing this song while on a tour of Kerry, provoking a row in the circus tent during which he was struck on the head with an iron bar. The blow proved fatal. Between the Monday, when he was injured and taken to O'Sullivan's Hotel in Tralee, and the following Thursday, when he was taken to Tralee Fever Hospital, his condition continued to deteriorate. He died in the Fever Hospital on 31 May 1889, at the age of forty-nine, and is buried in the New Cemetery in Tralee. A memorial plaque was unveiled on his grave in 1985.

11.

Captain Francis O'Neill, Collector and Police Chief – Jigs, Reels and Cops

When traditional musicians meet to play, discuss and evaluate the myriad jigs, reels, hornpipes, marches and airs in the vast repertoire of Irish traditional music, inevitably the name of Captain Francis O'Neill is mentioned. O'Neill, who died in 1936 in Chicago, left a wealth of tunes, many of which were published for the first time after his death, as his legacy. His intention was to preserve these tunes for posterity, and they are kept alive by traditional musicians today. It is truly amazing to think that the bulk of his collected melodies were taken down by Irish immigrants like himself, in the city of Chicago in the early years of the last century.

Francis O'Neill was born on 28 August 1848 at Tralibane, just three miles from Bantry, a year after the worst famine year – 'Black '47'. The youngest of seven children, O'Neill grew up listening to pipers, fiddlers, and flute-players providing music for cross-road dances in the summer and farmhouse dances in the winter. He was taught to play the flute by neighbouring farmer Timothy Downing, who for some strange reason never taught Francis to read from musical notation, even though Downing possessed a large library of music manuscript. O'Neill was later to learn this skill, to a limited degree, in America. A good scholar with proficiency in Greek, Latin and mathematics, Francis O'Neill seemed destined to train as a teacher or to enter the church. However, at the age of sixteen he left Ireland, setting out as a cabin boy on an English merchant ship. He travelled the world, eventually settling in the United States of America, where he followed many careers, finally signing on as a Chicago policeman in 1873. He had a colourful career in the police force and was wounded in the back while trying to disarm a burglar during his first month on the beat. Because of his diligence, honesty, integrity, and ability to organise, Francis O'Neill was promoted to sergeant at the Deering Street Police Station in 1878. He married Anna Rogers and raised

Captain Francis
O'Neill, Chief of
Chicago Police from
1901–1905.

a family of ten children; he had five sons and five daughters. One daughter and all five sons died young. Three of his boys died on the same day from diphtheria while his eldest son, Rogers O'Neill, a promising musician and academic, died at the age of eighteen from spinal meningitis. It was Francis O'Neill's love for and interest in his native music that inspired him and gave him the strength to carry on collecting music following these tragic family losses.

O'Neill had already begun collecting tunes and fragments that he could recall from his youth in Tralibane. He soon discovered that the Chicago Police Department had a large number of Irish immigrants in its ranks, many of whom were fiddlers, pipers, and flute players – he was in his element.

At this time Francis O'Neill met another O'Neill, James O'Neill from County Down. James O'Neill was an accomplished fiddle player who possessed the talent that Francis O'Neill lacked – the ability to transcribe into manuscript form, with speed and accuracy, the tunes and songs of other performers. With Francis O'Neill's influence, a place in the police force was soon found for James O'Neill, and he eventually went on to attain the rank of sergeant. A lot of collecting was done in the Brighton Park area of Chicago where Sergeant O'Neill lived, and where there was a strong Irish population. Many families came forward because they remembered tunes and song airs from past times, which were then noted

Sergeant James O'Neill. He recorded all of the tunes in *O'Neill's Music of Ireland* in music manuscript.

down in the collection. Music manuscript collections were offered for assessment in the search for new or unusual tunes, and eventually approximately 3,000 tunes were gathered. The year 1903 saw the publication of *O'Neill's Music of Ireland, Eighteen Hundred and Fifty Melodies*, edited by Captain Francis O'Neill, arranged by James O'Neill and published by Lyon and Healy of Chicago. It contained 625 melodies that were classified as follows: Airs and Songs, 75 O'Carolan Compositions, 415 Double Jigs, 60 Single Jigs, 380 Reels, 225 Hornpipes, 20 Long Dances and 50 Marches and Miscellaneous Tunes. They were beautifully bound in maroon cloth with gold and green foil-blocking of the harp and shamrock motifs on the front and back covers.

After he retired from his job as Chief of Police in 1905 at the age of fifty-eight, Francis O'Neill devoted himself to collecting the many tunes from our musical heritage. Re-editing, assessing, and checking tunes to avoid duplication was a long and tedious process that culminated in another publication, *The Dance Music of Ireland, 1001 Gems, O'Neill's Irish Music, 250 Choice Selections arranged for Piano and Violin*, which appeared in 1908, with a new edition of *Popular Selections from O'Neill's Dance Music of Ireland* being published in 1910. The two-volume *Waifs and Strays of Gaelic Melody* appeared in 1922 and 1924.

Francis O'Neill not only collected and published the dance tunes of his native country, but also published two wonderful text books: *Irish Folk Music, a Fascinating Hobby* and *Irish Minstrels and Musicians* – invaluable reference material on traditional musicians that included photographs, poetry, and the history of the many tunes and airs in his other music publications.

Francis O'Neill, the Chicago Chief of Police from Tralibane, County Cork, did a great service to our native music with his wonderful work, ensuring the survival and preservation of one genre of Ireland's music, with almost all of his material gathered from the Irish in Chicago.

12.

Charles Villiers Stanford – A Man for All Seasons

The Complete Collection of Irish Music, as noted by George Petrie, edited by Charles Villiers Stanford, was published in October 1903. At last the full 1,574 tunes were made available to the public through the diligent toil of this eminent composer. Stanford wrote a short but interesting preface to the three volumes from which I quote:

The publication of the complete collection of Dr George Petrie's manuscript of Irish Music at last realizes the aspirations of those enthusiastic Irishmen, most of them no more, who founded in December, 1851, the 'Society for the Preservation and Publication of the Melodies of Ireland'. The Society only succeeded in printing one volume of Dr Petrie's work. The fact, however that the Society had at its disposal the materials of more than five such volumes, set me thinking how they could be traced and if possible published. My investigations happily resulted in the discovery of the material as it is now presented to the public exactly in the form which it took from Petrie's hand.

Stanford goes on to state that the copious notes made by Petrie would have to wait for another occasion for publication. Stanford may not be remembered in Ireland today, but as a nation we are deeply indebted to him for the editing and publication of George Petrie's wonderful extensive collection.

Charles Villiers Stanford was born on 30 September 1852 at No. 2 Herbert Street, Dublin, the only son of Mr and Mrs John Stanford. His father, a lawyer, was examiner in the Court of Chancery, Dublin and Clerk of the Crown, County Meath. Both parents were amateur musicians; John had a fine bass voice while his wife was an excellent pianist. The young Stanford received his early training in music from several teachers including R.M. Levey. A noted violinist, Levey had a keen interest

C.V. Stanford, born in 1852
at Herbert Street, Dublin.

in Irish traditional music, publishing two volumes of his collected work in his time. Stanford may have absorbed this interest and love for Irish folk-music from Levey, as became evident in his later musical compositions. It is no wonder that Charles Stanford composed a stirring march when he was only eight years old. Following his early education at the Henry Tilney Bassett School, Stanford was ready to move on.

Stanford studied music with Arthur O'Leary and Ernst Pauer in London, where his family had moved, in 1862. In 1870, at the age of eighteen, he won a scholarship to Queens College, Cambridge where he was taught composition and organ by Sir Robert Stewart. He moved to Trinity College in 1873 and succeeded J.L. Hopkins as college organist until 1892. On a sabbatical, following his graduation in 1874, Stanford travelled on the Continent where he studied composition in Leipzig with Carl Reinecke and with Friedrich Kiel in Berlin. Those travels afforded him the opportunity to listen to the 'new' music of Wagner, Brahms, Meyerbeer, and Offenbach. He returned to England regularly to conduct the Cambridge University Musical Society Orchestra and Choir in works by the great masters and in his own edition of the St Matthew Passion.

Charles Stanford was simultaneously Professor of Music at Cambridge University and Professor of Composition at the Royal College of Music for

Stanford edited the *Complete Collection of Irish Music* by Dr George Petrie in 1903.

almost forty years. His professorship at the Royal College began with the founda-tion of the College in 1883 and he held both posts until his death. He was given the honorary degree of Mus.D at Oxford in 1883, and at Cambridge in 1888. Stanford was a gifted teacher and the list of his students reads like a who's who of British music, with eminent names like Ralph Vaughan Williams, Gustav Holst, Herbert Howells, Frank Bridge, George Butterworth, Ernst Moeran, Arthur Bliss, and Percy Grainger; the crème de la crème of English composers.

Like many great artists, Charles Villiers Stanford often showed signs of eccen-tricity, and his wife was witness to his 'ways'. As a student in Germany he met and married the singer Jennie Wetton in Leipzig. One of his many eccentricities was to play the overture to Mozart's *Marriage of Figaro* as his wife boiled his egg for breakfast. His mood and the vivacity of his playing determined whether he had a soft or hard-boiled egg! Lady Stanford (Stanford was knighted in 1902) often acted as peace-maker in her husband's many misunderstandings with Sir Hubert Parry, who had succeeded Sir George Grove as Director of the College in Cambridge. Relations with colleagues and rivals were often strained. Yet, as conductor of the Leeds Music Festival, he promoted up-and-coming composers and their new works.

During his student days at Cambridge, Stanford championed the role of the organ and choral singing at the university. His great volume of sacred music was the foundation of the Anglican tradition. Pieces such as 'When in our music, God is glorified' and 'O Praise God in His Holiness' are still in the Hymn and Psalm Book. At times his Celtic roots came to the surface in his arrangements of traditional Irish melodies for his hymns. It was Stanford who inspired the revival of church music that had flourished at an earlier period under George Frederick Handel. As an organist himself, Stanford focused a lot of his church music on this great instrument of so many tonal colours.

He wrote music in many genres, from compositions for woodwind to full orchestral and choral works. As a composer, Stanford is regarded as the most influential in England in the latter half of the nineteenth century – he led the field in this renaissance of music. Among his compositions are 'Sonata for Clarinet and Piano', 'Clarinet Concerto', 'Fantasia and Toccata in D Minor for Organ', twelve 'Occasional Preludes for Organ', numerous choral works and services, three 'Motets for Un-Accompanied Choir', and a 'Stabat Mater for Soloist, Choir and Orchestra'. His seven symphonies, all written between 1876 and 1911, and his 'Irish Rhapsodies No.1 and No. 4' were written between 1901 and 1923. His greatest vocal accomplishment was the 'Requiem', which was not appreciated in his lifetime, but has begun to be recognized as one of the great Victorian masterpieces in this genre.

Charles Villiers Stanford, born in Dublin in 1852, died in London on 29 March, 1924. His ashes are buried in Westminster Abbey.

13.

Victor August Herbert – 'Ah! Sweet Mystery of Life'

'Ah! Sweet Mystery of Life!' is a song from the famous musical film and stage show *Naughty Marietta* that instantly brings to mind the singing of Jeanette MacDonald and Nelson Eddy. This is just one of many songs composed by Dublin-born Victor August Herbert, who composed no less than forty-three operettas during his musical career. Herbert was a prolific composer of over 230 works ranging from opera, cantata, symphonic, cello, piano, violin, brass band, choral and vocal works.

Victor August Herbert was born on 1 February 1859 in Dublin to Edward Herbert and Fanny Lover. His father died when Victor was very young and he grew up in London with his grandfather, the celebrated novelist, poet, composer and painter Samuel Lover. In later years Herbert set several of his grandfather's poems to music, including 'Widow Macree' for men's voices and 'Sweet Harp of the Days', which Herbert dedicated to John McCormack.

Victor's mother later married German physician Dr Wilhelm Schmidt, and the family settled in Stuttgart. A talented musician, Victor played the piano but soon took up the cello and studied with Max Steinfritz at the Stuttgart Konservatorium. On completion of his studies he spent a year in the orchestra of Baron Paul von Derwies, a wealthy Russian aristocrat. He then moved on as soloist to the orchestra of Edvard Strauss (who had succeeded his brother Johann). This was great experience for Victor, and was later reflected in his operettas.

In 1881 Victor Herbert returned to Stuttgart to join the court orchestra. It was at this time that he met and married a soprano in the court opera, Therese Forster. They had a son, Gilbert, and a daughter, Ella. In 1886 the Herbert family immigrated to America where Therese sang the title role in the American premiere of Verdi's *Aida*, while Victor was principal cellist in the orchestra of the Metropolitan Opera House.

Another side of Victor Herbert's musical life was when he acted as conductor of the 22nd Regimental Band of the New York National Guard. He was involved with concert and marching bands until he once again changed direction, serving as conductor of the Pittsburgh Symphony from 1898 to 1902. He founded the Victor Herbert Orchestra six years later and conducted programmes of light orchestral music on tours and at summer resorts for many years.

In 1894 he composed the first of his forty-three operettas: *Prince Ananias*. This was quickly followed by *The Serenade, The Fortune Teller, Babes in the Wood, Madam'selle Modiste, The Red Mill*, and *Naughty Marietta*, making him one of the best-known figures in American music. Herbert's ambition was to compose an Irish operetta and he fulfilled it in 1917 with his operetta *Eileen*. A work in three acts with lyrics by Henry Blossom, set in 1798, its main title was 'The Hearts of Erin'. He also composed a major orchestral work with a strong Irish influence entitled *An Irish Rhapsody* for symphonic orchestra. In 1915 Victor Herbert became the first man to compose a film score for the – alas, forgotten – sequel to *The Birth of a Nation* entitled *The Fall of a Nation*.

Florenz Ziegfield, who was regarded as 'the greatest showman in theatrical history', in 1907 inaugurated the famous Ziegfield Follies at the Jardin de Paris in New York. Many composers contributed to these shows with new works, including Victor Herbert (with 'Can't You Hear Your Country Calling?', 'Legend of the Golden Tree' and 'Lady of the Lantern', among others). With so many songs, musicals and 'new' composers emerging, Victor Herbert foresaw that ownership and rights to musical compositions were slipping away from the composer into the public domain. He decided the champion the rights of composers and together with John Philip Sousa – the famous brass-band composer – and others, he founded the American Society of Composers, Authors and Publishers, ASCAP.

Thanks to his friendship with Thomas Edison, inventor of the phonograph, Victor Herbert was one of the first to record his music. He made and issued recordings of some of his works in orchestral versions, including 'Petite Waltz', 'American Fantasie' and 'Indian Summer'. Herbert left a wonderful legacy of music and song and was prolific despite his bad health. The 1939 film *The Great Victor Herbert* , a biographical look at the Irish-American composer's life and times, starred Walter Connolly, Mary Martin (*South Pacific*) and Allan Jones (*The Donkey Serenade*). The Naxos label issued a CD in 1999 entitled *Victor Herbert: Beloved Songs and Classic Miniatures*.

Victor August Herbert died of a heart attack on 26 May 1924 in New York, aged sixty-four.

14.

Patrick Joseph McCall: Musician, Poet and Balladeer

Patrick Joseph McCall, known as P.J., was the only surviving son of three children born to John and Eliza Mary McCall on 6 March 1861 at 25 Patrick Street, Dublin. Despite being born, bred and educated in the city, McCall was totally conversant with country life – its customs, habits, manners and histories all learned from his parents. John McCall was a native of Killalongford near Clonmore, County Carlow, while his wife, Eliza Mary Newport, came from Rathangan in the Barony of Bargy in south-east Wexford. At an early age P.J. showed an aptitude for writing, which was encouraged by his father, who was himself a prolific writer. On finishing his studies P.J. joined his father in the grocery and spirit business but he was never too far away from the quite extensive collection of historical, literary and biographical works in his father's library.

Each summer, in the company of his parents, the young P.J. visited Rathangan for holidays with his mother's people, the Newports. P.J. seemed to have enjoyed this time spent in the countryside filled with well-kept, white-washed, thatched homes, friendly neighbours, the sound of creaking sails of wind-mills, ruined castles and the lapping waves of the Atlantic Ocean on the nearby sandy beaches.

The McCalls eventually bought a cottage of their own, which survived until recent times, not far from the village cross-roads where they spent pleasant summer days. P.J. married Margaret Furlong, third daughter of James Walter Furlong, Knocklyon Lodge, Firhouse on 3 October 1900. Even after their marriage P.J. and his wife Margaret still visited Rathangan where much of his prolific poetic output was composed and written on the Cull Bank overlooking the sea. It was in this spot near the rolling sea that the many tunes learned or heard at 'last night's fun' were noted down in manuscript form. Rathangan, Duncormick and their environs were rich in history, folklore, music, tradition

an τατair seán ó murċú

Fr John Murphy of Boolavogue who led the insurgents in the 1798 Insurrection.

God grant you glory, brave Father Murphy,
And open heaven to all your men ;
The cause that called you may call to-morrow
In another fight for the Green again.

and the remnants of an almost forgotten language, Yola, which the ever-vigilant McCall noted down in the various notebooks he carried at all times. Evenings of visitors to his cottage and visitations by the McCalls to the surrounding neighbours brought delightfully pleasant hours of music, song, dance and story telling.

John McCall, P.J.'s father, was editor of several popular almanacs of the day, in particular *Old Moore's Almanack*. The young P.J. had some early verse published in this annual almanac, and following his father's death in his seventy-ninth year on 18 January 1902, P.J. McCall became editor of *Old Moore's Almanack*. P.J. would have been very aware of the worthy work his father carried out for the poor in his area in his capacity as board member of the Poor Law Guardians in the South Dublin Union to which his father was elected in 1880.

John McCall also served as a collector for the Sick and Indigent Roomkeepers' Society. P.J. McCall inherited many of his father's concerns for the poor of this ancient part of the city and played a role in the alleviation of the hardships suffered by the poor in Victorian Dublin.

A portrait of P.J. McCall, which appeared in *The Lamp* with a biography of the poet.

The McCall household at 25 Patrick Street was known as 'Poet's Hall' – where poets, writers, ballad-makers, historians and musicians of the time, local and visiting, gathered and were made welcome by the McCalls. This was the ideal environment for P.J. McCall to listen, absorb, and eventually to emulate the many talented people gathered there in his very home, a veritable treasure house of all things Gaelic. The seeds had been sown and very soon the writings, poetry and collected music of P.J. McCall would appear in the printed form.

In 1888 McCall became a member of the newly formed Pan-Celtic Society which was established in Dublin and whose members included W.B. Yeats, Douglas Hyde, and Maude Gonne. Up to that time McCall was unaware of having any real literary ability. The Pan-Celtic Society put him on the right track and he followed it without the least difficulty. Other members of this society included well-known literary figures Alfred Percival Graves, Katherine Tynan, and John and Ellen O'Leary.

Unfortunately, the Pan-Celtic Society was short-lived as it only existed for four years and was eventually superseded by The Irish National Literary Society. August 16 1892 was a very important date in the history of the Irish literary movement, with the formal inauguration of the Irish National Literary Society at a public meeting in the Rotunda, Dublin. Patrick Joseph McCall became the first Honorary Secretary of the newly-founded society and was surrounded by some of Ireland's most important and influential writers of the day. The proceedings were presided over by Charles Gavin Duffy, a veteran of the Young Ireland Movement and founding editor of *The Nation*, with Thomas Davis and John Dillon. The inaugural address was delivered by Dr George Sigerson. Elected officers were Dr Douglas Hyde, the Society's first president; Dr D.V. Coffey (later to become President of University College, Dublin) as treasurer; and Patrick Joseph McCall as secretary. McCall used the pen-name Cavellus (which he said was a Latin version of his surname, MacCathmhaoil or McCall) for many of his early writings.

It is the ballad compositions such as 'Kelly the Boy from Killann', 'Follow Me Up to Carlow', 'The Lowlands Low' and 'Boolavogue' written under his own name which immediately identify McCall and place him in the upper strata of national poets such as Thomas Davis, Samuel Ferguson, Robert Dwyer Joyce *et al*. His very descriptive and rousing ballad 'Boolavogue' was first printed in *The Irish Weekly Independent* on 18 June 1898 to commemorate the heroic deeds of Father John Murphy of Boolavogue on the centenary of the Insurrection of 1798. It was originally titled 'Father Murphy of the County Wexford' and sung to an entirely different melody than that of 'Youghal Harbour' to which it is now performed.

McCall had many of his works published when, in 1894, his collection of historical poems and ballads, translations from the Gaelic, humorous and characteristic sketches and miscellaneous songs entitled *Irish Nóiníns* (Daisies) was published. This collection contained the descriptive poem 'The Mummers of Bargy' and the humorous 'Tatter Jack Walsh', which may be sung to the jig of that name. In the same year McCall's historical account of the streets and characters of his own area of the Liberties was published and titled 'In the Shadow of St Patrick's'. Both publications received very favourable reviews in many journals of the day. Numerous volumes of poetry, ballads and humorous ditties flowed from the pen of McCall: 'Songs of Erin', 'Pulse of the Bards', 'The Harp at Home', 'Irish Street Ballads' and 'Irish Fireside Songs'. The books *Of Folklore Riddles* and *Leinster Localisms* as well as a volume of stories, *The Fenian Nights Entertainments*, were added to the list of his works. A second historical book, *In the Shadow of Christ Church*, appeared in 1899 together with a pamphlet on the life and times of Zozimus – the pseudonym of Michael Moran, the blind balladeer and singer who lived in Faddle Alley off Blackpitts in the Liberties *c.*1794, McCall's home territory.

From the foundation in 1893 of the Gaelic League, McCall was an enthusiastic worker and supporter of this new organisation whose aim was to foster, preserve and use the Irish language. There is every possibility that he was present at its inaugural meeting on 31 July 1893 and again at the meeting a few days later on 4 August during which Douglas Hyde was elected its president.

On his visits to Rathangan McCall encouraged the setting up of branches of the Gaelic League in the village and the neighbouring village of Duncormick. In 1894, with the cooperation of Dr Charles Villiers Stanford and Alfred Percival Graves, a committee was formed from representatives of the National Literary Society, the Gaelic League and the musical profession to organise a National Musical Festival, which was to become known as the Feis Ceoil. Dr Annie Patterson, an authority on Irish music, and P.J. McCall were the first Honorary Secretaries of this steering committee. In the early years of Feis Ceoil P.J. often acted as an adjudicator for the Irish ballad singing competition, donating a silver trophy for this competition, known as the P.J. McCall Cup, and still competed for today. In 1914 McCall, in conjunction with Arthur Darley, published a collection of melodies entitled 'Feis Ceoil Collection of Airs'.

Patrick Joseph McCall entered the political arena by seeking election as a councillor on Dublin Corporation representing the Wood Quay Ward. He was duly elected to the Corporation in 1897 and again in 1902, so overall he served a total of fifteen years representing the Wood Quay Ward on Dublin Corporation. During those years McCall worked tirelessly for the poor and under-privileged residents of Patrick Street, Nicholas Street, Winetavern Street, Lord Edward Street, Bull Alley, Bride Street, Golden Lane, Werburgh street, Francis Street, the Coombe, Wood Quay and a myriad of small streets, lanes and alleys that made up this area of the Liberties. Architecturally, the entire area is dominated by the looming edifice of Dublin Castle and lies in the shadows of St Patrick's and Christ Church cathedrals. McCall was very much aware of the plight of his constituents and represented them and their needs, taking their cause to the highest levels of authority, including to a Parliamentary Committee at Westminster, London, to contest the proposed St Patrick's Park Bill. Most of his clinics were held at 25 Patrick Street, where his father had started his business on 3 March 1856, and which continued until P.J. retired because of ill-health (he suffered from chronic arthritis) in 1918. Father and son spent a proud sixty-two years involved in the commercial life of the area, never ceasing to care for and represent those less fortunate.

Retiring to a new home, Westpoint in Sutton, McCall continued to write during his last days, completing a short play for publication in the Feis Carman programme of 1919. It was while watching an airplane fly over the hill of Howth on its approach for landing at Dublin Airport that McCall took seriously ill. He lived but a short time after this, departing this world on his birthday, 6 March 1919. His remains were interred in Glasnevin cemetery. McCall's songs and ballads go into the hundreds. Within these poems we find many fine examples of Irish *goltraí, geantraí agus suantraí*. He had an intimate knowledge of local traditions, legends, history, music, dance and the life of those with whom he spent many happy days in the summer sun of long ago.

A bronze sculpture of five pikemen, commemorating the Battle of the Three Rocks outside of Wexford town.

15.

Margaret Burke Sheridan – Maggie from Mayo

Margaret Burke Sheridan was one of the leading sopranos of the 1920s and despite her relatively short operatic career she endeared herself to Italian audiences. Margarita Sheridan, as she was known in Italy, was born the youngest of seven children, on 15 October 1889 at the Mall in Castlebar, County Mayo. Her house was once the local post office, where her father served as post master at the time. Margaret was orphaned at the age of four when both her parents died, and for the next five years she lived with friends in Newtown, Castlebar.

Through an arrangement between local parish priest Canon Lyons and Mother Peter McGrath, prioress of the Dominican Convent, Eccles Street, Dublin, Margaret Burke Sheridan began her studies with the Dominicans. By this time she had adopted her father's second name, Burke, in his memory. It was at Eccles Street Convent that Margaret received her first music lessons from Mother Clement. She showed exceptional talent and in 1908 won a Gold Medal at the Dublin Feis Ceoil. Another famous singer in a different vocal genre, Delia Murphy, was also a student at the Dominican Convent and struck up a lifelong friendship with Margaret. It was felt that Margaret should have the opportunity to study in London, and with that in mind a sponsored concert was organized to raise the fees needed for her to attend the Royal Academy of Music there.

While in London Margaret met her godfather and family friend, T.P. O'Connor MP, who was a great help to her – as was Lady Randolph Churchill, mother of the future prime minister, Winston. At a musical soirée in one of London's fashionable houses, Margaret and her singing made a great impression on Guglielmo Marconi, the inventor of wireless telegraphy, who invited her to continue her career in Italy. He made the necessary arrangements and introductions for her to study singing with Alfredo Martini and Emma Correlli in Rome. Martini was very critical of Sheridan – when he heard her sing Madam Butterfly's opening aria he exclaimed: 'You have a wonderful voice, but you don't know the first thing about singing'. She worked hard, however, and her total dedication resulted in her making her operatic debut in *La Constanzia* to great acclaim.

The great conductor Arturo Toscanini heard her and invited her to sing the role of Mimi in Puccini's *La Bohème*. Her outstanding performance led to a long series of successful engagements in operas by Puccini. She made her London debut at Covent Garden in 1919 singing the title role of Mimi in *La Bohème*. She also appeared in the first London performance of Mascagni's *Iris*.

Returning to Italy, Margarita Sheridan enjoyed great success. She sang and recorded with such notable tenors as Aureliano Pertile and Beniamino Gigli and also partnered the Chilean singer Renato Zanelli in many operatic performances together with baritones Carlo Galeffi, Dennis Noble, and Giovanni Inghilleri and the famous basso buffo, Salvatore Baccaloni.

La Margarita was at the pinnacle of her career when she performed at La Scala, Milan, with Toscanini conducting. She sang the title role of Catalani's *La Wally* in 1922 and in 1923 sang the role of Candida in the world premiere of Respighi's *Belfagor*. She was coached personally by Puccini for the title role in *Manon Lescaut*, which was to become her most successful role. It was at La Scala that the then Archbishop of Milan heard her sing and remarked, 'heaven came very near when I heard her singing'. Following his elevation to pontiff as Pope Pius XI, he offered Margaret Burke Sheridan the title of Countess, which with great modesty and humility she declined.

Margaret Burke Sheridan never married but at one stage in her career fell in love and became engaged to an Italian count. The entire engagement fell through, however, when she found out that he was already a married man. In 1934 she suffered a severe illness and lost her confidence, particularly because of her inability to reach her own very high artistic standards.

To the great disappointment of her many musical compatriots and her multitude of fans and followers, Margaret retired from singing and returned to Dublin in 1935. She was forty-six years of age. At the invitation of the New York Foundation of Opera, she went to America in 1950 to be an advisor in the search for new operatic vocal talent and worked with eminent conductors like Bruno Walter and Serge Koussevitsky, with composer Ralph Vaughan Williams, and with her old friend Ezio Pinza, the world famous bass. She never sang in America.

Back in Dublin she broadcast a series of biographical-style programmes on Radio Eireann, recounting her life and operatic experiences. In 1949, in her sixtieth year, she made a series of gramophone recordings with an orchestra under the musical direction and baton of Terry O'Connor. The recordings were made at the Aula Maxima in UCD (University College Dublin) which is now the National Concert Hall. Margaret was relatively satisfied with these, but her many musical friends expressed disappointment with the previews they listened to. These made Sheridan doubt their artistic and musical merit, and as a result these recordings were not made available to the public until after her death. Margaret continued to live in Dublin up to the time of her final illness and death, which occurred at St Vincent's Hospital on 16 April 1958, at the age of sixty-nine.

One of the songs she recorded at the Aula Maxima was Thomas Moore's 'When He Who Adores Thee', which showed up some of the wonderful vocal qualities of Margaret Burke Sheridan's beautiful voice. Dubbed 'the Empress of Ireland' by Toscanini, she will always be known to us as Maggie from Mayo.

16.

Leo Rowsome – Rí na bPíobairí

Rí na bPíobairí was the title conferred on Leo Rowsome by his contemporaries – in recognition, not only of his wonderful piping skills, but also of his expertise and craftsmanship in the intricate work involved in manufacturing and repairing uilleann pipes. Leo Rowsome's sound was instantly recognizable. Clear, vibrant, and perfectly pitched tones filled even the largest concert hall. His regulator, or keyed accompaniment, was truly amazing, and added to the overall effect of the music by clever and expert use of the harmonic notes available to him. One of the best examples of his wonderful piping can be heard in Leo's rendition of Edward Keating Hyland's descriptive composition *The Fox Chase*. The sport of the chase is captured by the chanter, or main melody pipe, accompanied by the well-tuned drones, which give a constant unison note across the three drone pipes, with the harmonic interjection of the chordal sounds produced by the regulators. Here was Rowsome at his very finest. Leo Rowsome's rendition of this small suite of traditional tunes brought laughter, applause and cheers of appreciation from all who were privileged to hear a live concert performance, as he mimicked the sounds of the hounds, horses and the unfortunate Reynard in his final death throes. Encouraging chants of 'Good man, Leo' and *ar aghaidh leat* were always part of the vocal accompaniment to his mesmerizing performance. Who was this Leo Rowsome?

The Rowsome family was originally from Ballintore, Wexford, where they farmed quite extensively. Samuel Rowsome was the first family member to take up playing the uilleann pipes and he started a piping dynasty that has survived to the fifth generation with the playing and pipe-making of Kevin Rowsome, who lives in Dublin. Samuel Rowsome was a contemporary of John Cash, the travelling piper, and Jemmy Byrne, the piper from Shanagarry, County Carlow, both of whom played at the annual Fair of Scarawalsh near Enniscorthy. The Rowsomes

John Rowsome, uileann piper, of Ballintore, Ferns, Co. Wexford.

were taught music in Ferns by a German musician, Jacob Blowitz, who gave them a good grounding in the theory and reading of musical notation. This musical education was a great asset for future generations of Rowsome pipers.

William Rowsome, Leo's father, moved from Ferns to live in and set up an uilleann pipe-making workshop in Dublin, which proved very productive and popular in the bustling metropolis. Pipers from all over Ireland visited Willie Rowsome's workshop to search for a new set of pipes, repair existing pipes or to get chanter, regulator, or drone reeds. Rowsome was the expert reed-maker. Without good reeds the uilleann pipes' musical voice is non-existent. Properly cured and prepared, split and shaped Spanish cane with a perfectly fitted staple allows the ebony wood chanter to speak. This service was much sought after by the piping fraternity and these were the special skills handed down to the young Leo Rowsome by his father.

It was as a violinist that Leo commenced his musical career that was to span a lifetime. He soon moved on to the uilleann pipes, leaving the violin-playing to his brother, Tom. Leo seemed to possess a natural gift for playing the extremely difficult and temperamental uilleann pipes: the player has to operate a wind-bag, filled by a bellows placed under the armpits of each arm, while using the fingers of each hand to extract the musical notes from the melody pipe or chanter and at the same time using the heel of the right hand to punch the regulator keys that provide the harmonic accompaniment. A daunting task indeed!

Soon, reels like 'The Dogs Among the Bushes', 'Trim the Velvet', 'The Bucks of Orranmore' and fine jigs like 'Tatter Jack Walsh', 'The Gold Ring', 'The Old Grey Goose' and the awkward hornpipe known as 'The Independence' were leaping from the concert pitch chanter, under the dexterous fingers of master piper Leo Rowsome. Leo was in demand at concerts, *feiseanna* and piping festivals the length and breadth of Ireland, with many trips overseas to England, Scotland, Wales, the Continent, and America, where he performed at Carnegie Hall.

As well as being a performer of the highest standard, Leo Rowsome was also a fine teacher, and he taught with great dedication at the Municipal School of Music for over thirty-four years. Among his pupils were Paddy Moloney (of the Chieftains), Liam O'Flynn, and Willie Clancy, from Milltown Malbay. Leo also taught at The Piper's Club in Thomas Street on Saturday nights, and took part in the musical sessions for which this club was famous: the cream of Ireland's traditional musicians came to The Piper's Club for sessions and for the honour of playing with Leo Rowsome. This popular venue is long gone, but the sessions continue at Cultúrlann na hÉireann in Monktown every Saturday night, in a club named after Leo Rowsome.

Leo was making 78 rpm recordings from the 1920s, and his definitive album, 'Rí na bPíobairí', featuring a track of the same name, was launched by Claddagh Records in 1966. This album is a masterpiece of piping, with Leo playing both the concert-pitched and flat-pitched uilleann pipes. This album, now available on CD, is a 'must-have' for lovers of the pipes.

Leo also broadcast from 2 RN and Radio Eireann as a soloist and as the leader of the Rowsome Pipes Quartet. Under studio conditions it is difficult to keep the pipes in tune for a soloist – so imagine the task of tuning four sets of pipes to sound as one, considering the complexities of the delicate reeds and the effects of fluctuating temperatures. It was the reeds used and made by Leo that made this possible. The result of this was wonderful and enjoyed and marvelled at by those who listened to those broadcasts with rapt attention. Members of the quartet over the years were Leo's brother Tom, Willie Clancy, Tommy Reck (from Oylgate, County Wexford), Seán Seery, Dave Page, Eddie Potts (from Duncormuck, County Wexford), Michael Touhy, and of course Leo's son, the late Leon Rowsome, also a fine piper and pipe-maker.

Today, we have a multitude of CDs of uilleann pipers performing as soloists and in groups and ensembles, playing wonderful selections of the most intricately ornamented tunes. In his time, Rowsome was one of a hand-full of uilleann pipers available on disc, most of which were breakable wax recordings, and if they survived the ravages of being ploughed to death by a steel gramophone needle, they were almost inaudible anyway. We are fortunate that many of Leo Rowsome's wonderful recordings are still available, due to the advances of modern technology in restoring older recordings. Leo Rowsome's tutor book for the uilleann pipes was one of the first and longest-surviving DIY books for the pipes. During his lifetime, Leo amassed quite a collection of tunes in manuscript form, including some of his own compositions, which were published by Walton's Music Galleries and included some 428 reels and jigs from this collection.

Leo died suddenly while adjudicating at the Fiddler of Dooney competition in Sligo in 1970, depriving the world of traditional music of one of its Master Musicians - *Rí na bPíobairí*.

This tradition is still extant today in the person of Kevin Rowsome, a fifth generation piper, who received his early piping lessons from his grandfather Leo and later from his own father, the late Leon Rowsome.

17.

Jimmy Kennedy – South of the Border

How many times have you heard these opening lines: 'If you go down to the woods today/You're sure of a big surprise/ If you go down in the woods today/ You'd better go in disguise/ For every bear that ever there was / Will gather there for certain, because/ Today's the day the teddy bears have their picnic'? You wonder, 'I wonder who wrote that song?' Well, the answer is simple – an Irishman by the name of Jimmy Kennedy. Jimmy wrote the words to music that had already been composed by American musician John K. Bratton in 1907, and originally called 'Teddy Bears' Two-Step'.

This is only one of approximately 2,000 songs written by Jimmy Kennedy, the prolific songwriter from Northern Ireland. He was born on 20 July 1902 in Omagh, County Tyrone, and grew up in Portstewart, County Derry. He received his formal education at Trinity College, Dublin, and later spent some time teaching in England. Following the success of 'The Teddy Bears' Picnic', which sold over four million copies on record, Jimmy decided to write songs full-time.

Jimmy Kennedy became part of London's Tin Pan Alley, which was actually Denmark Street; this was where the most important music publishers, music agents, composers and lyricists had their offices. (Originally, Tin Pan Alley was the nickname given to an actual street in Manhattan: West 28th Street, between Broadway and Sixth Avenue where many of the music publishers had their offices). Kennedy was a lyricist who, in partnership with a musician or composer, co-wrote the songs. At that time, in the early 1900s, the popularity of a song was reliant on the number of copies of the sheet music for voice and piano that were sold, so it was important for it to appeal sufficiently to audiences for them to buy the sheet music.

One of Kennedy's most successful song-writing partnerships was with Michael Carr. In 1931, 'The Barmaid's Song', sung by Lancashire music-hall singer Gracie Fields, became an instant hit for Jimmy Kennedy. Many of his songs began their

Jimmy Kennedy's 'South of the Border' was recorded by singing cowboy Gene Autry (1907-1998).

lives in Ireland, as evidenced by 'Red Sails in the Sunset', which was inspired by a small yacht that Jimmy watched as it sailed westward into the setting sun off Portstewart. While driving in a dense fog, his car's headlights picked out a sign that read ' Harbour Lights', which ended up being the title of another hit song. A newspaper headline about the singer Gracie Fields' holiday in Capri gave him the idea for the catchy ditty, 'The Isle of Capri'. His sister sent him a colourful post-card from Southern California, telling him, 'Today we've gone to Mexico, south of the border...' – and this inspired 'South of the Border, Down Mexico Way'. This song has been recorded by numerous international artists including cowboy star Gene Autry, and has sold millions of records over the years.

Kennedy was a very private and modest man who never really received the recognition he deserved in his lifetime. His lyrics were sung and recorded by countless performers, including Bing Crosby, Perry Como, Ella Fitzgerald, Nat 'King' Cole, Frank Sinatra, The Platters, Elvis Presley, Tony Bennett, Louis Armstrong, Roy Orbison, Tom Jones, Glenn Miller and many, many more. One of his biggest hits was 'My Prayer', which reached number two in the Hit Parade for The Platters, while his other song, 'South of the Border', was number one at the same time This was in 1939, and this feat was not equalled again until the sixties, by Lennon and McCartney.

During the Second World War, a dance craze called the 'Cokey, Cokey' swept across dance halls and is still popular today at parties and weddings and this was another Kennedy success. He had that happy knack of being able to put a story into a succinct lyric and match it to a catchy or memorable melody penned by one of his co-writers. He once overheard a conversation on a train in which a young lady was asked if her mother was Irish. This prompted Jimmy to pen 'Did Your Mother Come from Ireland?' a big hit in America that proved to be a major success for Bing Crosby. Crosby was friendly with Jimmy Kennedy and recorded no less than fourteen of the Omagh man's songs.

Though fame eluded Jimmy Kennedy during his lifetime, he did receive the Ivor Novello Award on two occasions, as well as an honorary Doctor of Literature from the New University of Ulster in 1978 and an OBE in 1983. Of the 2,000 or so songs written by Jimmy, 200 became worldwide hits, and 50 of them turned into evergreen popular classics. Songs like 'April in Portugal', 'Blaze Away', 'Home Town', 'Love Is Like a Violin', 'Play to Me', 'Gypsy,' 'Skye Boat Song', and 'We're Gonna Hang out our Washing on the Siegfried Line' are only some of the better-known of Jimmy Kennedy's many song titles.

This Irishman penned so many familiar favourites that have stood the test of time and the ravages of rock 'n' roll that he was posthumously inducted into the Songwriters Hall of Fame in 1997. He lived in Greystones, County Wicklow, for a time in the 1970s and later moved to Cheltenham, where he died on April 6, 1984. He is buried in Taunton, Somerset.

18.

Delia Murphy – 'If I Were a Blackbird'

I've been a Moonshiner for many a year/ I've spent all my money on whiskey and beer/ I'll go to some hollow and set up my still/ I'll make you a gallon for a two dollar bill/ I'm a rambler, I'm a gambler…

Written by Delia Murphy, this song has been sung where many a glass was raised in celebration at home or abroad – everyone knows the chorus, at least.

Delia Murphy was born on 16 February 1902 at Mount Jennings, Hollymount, near Claremorris in County Mayo. Her father made his fortune in the gold and silver mines of North America, and on his return to Ireland he bought Mount Jennings, a two-storey Georgian house at Hollymount. It was here that Delia grew up with her one brother and six sisters, playing in the extensive grounds of the house. Childhood was idyllic. Delia's love of music and her fascination with traditional music began at an early age. It was forbidden to speak Irish in school, but Delia broke with this rule at playtime and on the way home from school, speaking and singing many songs in the Irish language. As a young girl, Delia developed a friendship with Tom Maughan, a traveller whose family was encamped in Featherbed Lane, near her home. It's said that it was from Tom Maughan and his family that Delia picked up some of her songs and ballads.

Delia had a great memory for song lyrics and could sing song after song without reference to any texts or prompt sheets. She also composed some songs herself, including the famous 'Three Lovely Lassies in Bannion', 'Dance with Me', 'County Tyrone', 'The Captain with the Whiskers', 'The Moonshiner', and 'Dan O'Hara', the poignant story of the poor old farmer who fell on hard times and resorted to selling boxes of matches to eke out a living. Delia would sing around the house, honing and fine-tuning her songs and ballads to her own liking, ensuring she expressed every sentiment contained in the lyrics. She loved to discover new songs and add them to her repertoire, and seemed to specialize for the most part in cheerful songs.

Following secondary level, Delia Murphy entered University College Galway, where she studied Commerce. One of her lecturers was Thomas Kiernan, an assistant inspector of taxes and part-time lecturer. They met formally at a wedding party, where he agreed to accompany Delia while she sang after the wedding, and love blossomed. They married in 1924 at University Church, St Stephen's Green, Dublin. Neither family attended the wedding as they did not approve of the match, both families thinking their child was marrying beneath them.

Delia was the only child in her family to matriculate and graduate from university. As her new husband had also been her teacher at UCG, his parents thought Delia too young for their son. After their marriage the Kiernans moved to London, where Thomas began his career as a diplomat in the High Commission and Delia was expected to play the role of the diplomat's wife.

Both of the Kiernans played a big role in promoting Ireland and all things Irish while Thomas served in London, in the challenging role of diplomat to an English government still unfamiliar and uncomfortable with Irish independence. Delia often sang at the National University of Ireland Club in London, which her husband helped establish, and which created Irish cultural traditions there. It may have been Delia's exile in London that provided her with the opportunity to develop her talent as a ballad singer. The songs that Delia sang were purely Irish, nationalistic, and characterised by sing-a-long style choruses, which provided her audience with a 'hands-on' chance to join the chorus – which most people enjoy. We must remember that at the time, opera or English drawing-room music was the norm, while Delia Murphy entertained audiences in a celebration of all things Irish.

It was in 1935 that the Kiernans returned to Ireland, where Thomas became director of programmes for Radio Eireann. At this time, just before the Second World War, Delia established herself as an Irish folk-singer and recorded her best-known songs: 'If I Were a Blackbird', 'The Spinning Wheel', and 'Three Lovely Lassies in Bannion', which were taken to a wider audience through the medium of the gramophone. She was in her thirties, married with four children, and seemed a most unlikely singing star. She had been singing all her life, with impromptu appearances only for family and friends in diplomatic circles, but when she recorded for HMV her singing career took off. She sold thousands of 78rpm records and delighted her many new fans with songs like 'The Boston Burglar', 'Hello, Patsy Fagan', 'I Was Told By My Aunt', 'Let Him Go, Let Him Tarry' and her two big favourites, 'The Spinning Wheel' and 'If I Were a Blackbird', and also became popular with songs that she composed herself. From 1950 to 1954, Delia sang in many venues in England and Ireland, including a St Patrick's Day Concert in London in 1951, which was recorded by Radio Eireann. Delia Murphy died in 1971, leaving many memories for those who enjoyed her performances in concerts and in recordings. Her songs are still very much alive today, and on the centenary of her birth in 2002, a memorial plaque was unveiled on a farm building on the site of her old home:

> If I were a blackbird I'd whistle and sing,
> I would follow the ship that my true love sails in,
> And in the top rigging I would there build my nest,
> And I'd pillow my head on his lily white breast.

19.

John Feeney – Moonlight in Mayo

'Oh, why do I dream and think about Ireland? I tried to forget, but I was wrong,
Always despondent - till one fine evening, I heard Jack Feeney sing a song.'

These are the opening lines of a poem composed by Shaun O'Nolan – a Wicklow piper and tenor who recorded traditional music and song in New York in the 1920s – in praise of his hero, Irish-American tenor John Feeney.

John or Jack Feeney was born over a century ago, on 9 August 1903 in Swinford, County Mayo. One of Patrick and Mary Feeney's seven children, John was educated locally, finishing his education in 1919 at the age of sixteen. John excelled at singing while at school and his mother arranged for piano lessons with the local church organist. Following a short spell serving in the family shop in Swinford, John Feeney followed his older brother, Pat, to London and worked for McAlpine on the building of Wembley Stadium. In 1928 John set sail for America on board the *SS Samaria*, landing in New York on 11 June. His ambition: to have his tenor voice trained and to become a professional singer.

The Irish tenor enjoyed great popularity in America with such notable performers as William Scanlan, Andrew Mack, Chauncey Alcott and contemporary stars like Fiske O'Hara, Morton Downey and, of course, John McCormack. McCormack, who was acknowledged as one of the world's most popular and highest-paid entertainers of the time, was at the peak of his career in the 1920s.

In McCormack, John Feeney had an ideal role model and within five years of his arrival in New York he had made great strides in the music world. Feeney ranked very highly in a list of seventeen tenors performing in the New York area as outlined by the music critic of the *Gaelic American* newspaper. The six-foot tall, brown-haired, blue-eyed Mayo man had arrived with the recording of his

A portrait of John Feeney
from Swinford, Co. Mayo,
who was a born tenor.

first 78rpm disc on the Crown label called 'That's How I Spell Ireland'. It was recorded and released in New York in December 1931 and was followed by seven other songs recorded in two sessions.

Following the Depression in America, when all forms of entertainment were affected and record sales also faced a massive slump, Jack Kapp auditioned John Feeney for the Decca record label and his first recordings were issued at the end of 1934, aimed specifically at the lucrative Irish-American market. A song about his home place sung by a Mayo man, 'Moonlight in Mayo' became John's biggest popular hit with many of his fans, who were of the opinion that the song had been penned by John himself. The song had, in fact, been written by two Tin Pan Alley songsmiths – Percy Wenrich and Jack Mahoney – in 1914 and had been used in a play called *Kilkenny*.

The Decca label had engaged the very best orchestral players for these record-ings and under the baton of Victor Young, provided warm and rich orchestral effects to accompany John's ever-improving Irish tenor voice. Songs such as

A relaxed photograph of Jack, as he was generally known to his friends and family.

'The Garten Mother's Lullaby', 'That Old Irish Mother of Mine', 'Ballymoney', 'The Old House' and 'There's an Echo of Old Ireland Everywhere' soon became favourites with the Irish in America. The last title was the only song Feeney ever composed – with co-writers Dick Sandford and Nat Osborne, in 1937.

The advent of radio in the 1920s in America changed the music business completely, with at least fifty per cent of American families owning a radio set by the 1930s. This was perfect for John Feeney, for he was soon in big demand with the Irish-American listeners. John broadcast regularly on WINS's *Songs of Ireland* programme, which was broadcast on Sunday afternoons at half past three. Helen Merchant was John's piano accompanist for these broadcasts, which had a huge listenership.

It was when a German-American brewery – F.&M. Schaefer Brewing Co. of Brooklyn – auditioned for an Irish tenor for their radio programme that John Feeney's selection and subsequent success propelled the tenor from Swinford into 'big-time' radio broadcasting.

This is a publicity shot of Feeney holding a glass of Schaeffer beer, which he advertised on their sponsored radio show.

With Leo Reisman's Orchestra, Feeney's lyric tenor voice came over the air waves singing 'Killarney' during the St Patrick's Day Schaefer Revue. Many of these broadcast discs have survived, and restored excerpts may be heard on the two commemorative CDs produced on the Viva Voce label by Harry Bradshaw. Like many artists, John Feeney performed at the famed Carnegie Hall to a full house, as well as in Hotel Barbizon-Plaza, with the journals and music magazines of the day giving high praise to the young tenor from Mayo. The music critic for the *New York Times* wrote: 'With this auspicious start we, too, feel that the Mayo Nightingale has ascended the first rung of the ladder that will carry him to greater vocal heights in the future.'

During these years John continued to work on his vocal technique and extended his repertoire with vocal coaching from Bill Torner, Madame Orelli, and a teacher by the name of Phillips. The success of this training was very evident from the format of John's concert programmes, with Art Songs by George Frideric Handel, German *Lieder* by Franz Schubert and Robert Franz and operatic arias by Purcell and Puccini. The second half of John's concert comprised a well-chosen selection of Irish favourites. This was a winning formula that took John Feeney to the upper echelons of recitalists.

Feeney with James
McCormack at the
piano. James was
the brother of Irish
tenor John Count
McCormack.

John and his wife Maura made several working trips home to Ireland. In 1935 he appeared at Dublin's Olympia Theatre and this concert was broadcast on 2RN. On 1 September of that year he 'topped the bill' at a Celebrity Concert at the Town Hall, Swinford, organised by St Joseph's Choral Society. In 1937 John gave performances at Dublin's Theatre Royal, the Cork Opera House and the Savoy Cinema in Limerick, all to critical acclaim. While visiting Dublin John took singing lessons from Dr Vincent O'Brien, who had been John McCormack's first teacher.

Following the Second World War – in which John played a considerable role boosting public morale with his radio broadcasts – he made his last appearance in Dublin, in 1960. The occasion was a special broadcast to the United States on the eve of St Patrick's Day and featured many well-known Irish performers of the time.

In 1964, as he approached his sixtieth birthday, John decided to retire from singing. His health was beginning to fail, as he had minor heart problems. His wife Maura had inherited her father's thriving business, and with John purchasing a directorship, the couple returned to Ballina as owners of Messrs Hugh Ruddy & Co. Ltd – mineral water manufacturers.

The piano copy of 'When It's Moonlight in Mayo', Feeney's most requested song.

Early in 1967 John suffered a heart attack from which he recovered, but while returning to Ballina by car one day, John was startled by stray horses on the road. The car swerved to avoid the horses and ended up in a ditch at the side of the road. The shock brought on a massive heart attack that killed John Feeney, who died in Maura's arms on the roadside near Lough Talt on 22 December, 1967.

Maura Feeney later lived in an apartment in Ballsbridge, having sold the family business in 1976. In 1986 she returned to the United States and died in Florida in August 1990. Her ashes are buried with John in the Ruddy family grave.

While living in Dublin Maura had made contact with Harry Bradshaw, an expert in the restoration of sound recordings of traditional musicians such as Michael Coleman and James Morrison. A very reluctant Harry Bradshaw took away five huge cartons of acetate discs, concert programmes, sheet music, and other memorabilia of John Feeney's, claiming that this type of music really wasn't his forte. The cartons slumbered in Mr Bradshaw's attic for over twenty years, emerging in August 2003, the centenary of John Feeney's birth. His music was given a new lease of life on a wonderful 2-CD collection painstakingly restored by Mr Bradshaw. Maura Feeney had told him: 'If you don't take these cartons, Mr Bradshaw, they are bound for the refuse skip'. Thankfully, Harry Bradshaw beat the dustman to that particular collection.

20.

Johnny Doran – Travelling Piper

When his high-throated chanter and pipes gave a squall,
They were like a screech owl or a black-bird's sweet call!
Why, Mozart or Beethoven wasn't in it at all,
With this man called Johnny Doran the piper.

'Johnny Doran, a famous piper', reads the inscription on a headstone in Trinity Cemetery in Rathnew, County Wicklow. A simple statement, but as anyone interested in the uilleann pipes knows, this is the final resting place of one of the greatest pipers Ireland ever produced. Johnny Doran was, unusually, a member of the travelling people.

In the history of uilleann piping there were many 'gentleman' pipers in the eighteenth and nineteenth centuries; mostly landed gentry with an interest in Irish native music and a flair for playing the uilleann pipes. They included Lord Edward Fitzgerald ('the Patriot'), Pierce Power of Glynn, Lawrence Grogan of Johnstown Castle in Wexford, Walter Jackson of Ballingarry in Limerick, Capt. William Kelly of New Abbey House in Kildare, Henry Brownrigg of Norrismount in Wexford, and Dudley Colclough of Tintern Abbey. These men lived in pleasant homes on fine estates, while Johnny Doran was a travelling piper who strayed through the meadows and highways and byways of Ireland.

If one were to imagine a man of slight build, handsome, dark-haired, well-dressed, standing approximately five feet six inches in height, with a ready smile showing firm white teeth, soft-spoken and gentle with an easy-going manner, one would have some idea of what Johnny Doran was like. Johnny was born in 1908 into a family of five daughters and four sons to John and Kathleen Doran of Rathnew, County Wicklow. It is easy to see where Johnny got his passion for piping: it came down from his father, John Doran, who was a very fine piper himself.

The art of piping was also passed down to him from John Cash, the celebrated nineteenth-century Wexford piper, who was his maternal great-grandfather.

John Doran eventually taught his son Johnny to play the pipes, ensuring that this great tradition would carry on. Johnny in turn taught his younger brother Felix to play the pipes. Old John Doran was playing on a Dublin street one day when he was complimented on his fine playing by a passer-by and quickly responded, 'You should hear my two sons, Johnny and Felix'. Many interested musicians and listeners did hear them, because Johnny Doran played at practically every fair and race meeting the length and breadth of Ireland. His brother Felix followed in his foot-steps some years later. Anyone who heard Johnny play was immediately entranced by his style: fast-flowing, ornamented piping – you almost *had* to dance. The Galway step-dancer Paddy Philbin remembers hearing Johnny for the first time, as he played outside his caravan on a fine evening; he was so taken aback by Johnny's piping that he 'hadn't a step'. On becoming friends with Johnny, Paddy often danced to his music outside the Imperial Hotel in Galway, where Johnny always played on a Saturday evening when in the area.

Local musicians who lived in places that Johnny visited became firm and fast friends of his as he tripped out their favourite tunes: 'Rakish Paddy', 'The Steam Packet', 'Tarbolton', 'Colonel Frazier' and his favourite reel, 'The Swallow's Tail'. Martin Talty, Martin Rochford, Sean Reid, and of course the great Willie Clancy from Miltown Malbay played a lot of music with Johnny, following him on his travels through their native County Clare. It was Doran who introduced Willie Clancy to the finer points of playing, and what happened? Willie became famous in the musical world for his piping.

Johnny Doran played out in the open most of the time, always standing up and using the pipes box to rest his foot on and give him the elevation required to rest the regulators and drones across his knee. The older pipers used a forked stick as a crutch to achieve the same effect when playing standing up.

Johnny's open-air recitals were his means of support for wife and family, and his virtuoso playing ensured that the coffers were always full. Unlike other Travellers who used the barrel-shaped caravan as transport, Johnny Doran used a large square-top caravan drawn by a big mare as it trundled through the countryside. He was also ahead of his time, because he always carried a racing bike strapped to the rear of the wagon – it was his means of travelling into towns to play gigs, and the drop handlebars on the racer were ideal for carrying his pipes.

Although Johnny Doran never practiced the trade of tinsmithing, he had the ability and dexterity to fashion chanter and regulator keys for his instrument from the bowls and handles of silver spoons. He would use the iron band of the caravan wheel as an anvil on which to tap out the new key. He made his reeds from Spanish cane, thereby keeping his pipes in tip-top condition.

During the Second World War, Johnny found it relatively easy to settle in Dublin, as the Piper's Club in Thomas Street was very active at that time and

Johnny Doran was a most welcome visitor at the musical sessions. One of the members, Clareman John Kelly, had a shop in Capel Street where Johnny was a regular visitor for the musical gatherings that were held there. It was John Kelly who arranged for Kevin Danaher of the Irish Folklore Commission to record Johnny Doran in December 1947. Johnny played ten selections at that session, for the princely sum of £1 per recording, and a tentative arrangement for Danaher to record further sessions was made. This, alas, was not to be. The recordings made on that evening are the only recordings of Johnny Doran, who died on 19 January 1950, after a long illness and hospitalization resulting from an accident. A wall had fallen on his parked caravan during a raging storm in early 1948, and Johnny suffered a broken back and other internal injuries that he never fully recovered from. The aforementioned recording is fortunately available on CD from Na Piobairi Uilleann, Henrietta Street, Dublin, to lovers of uilleann piping.

21.

Doctor at the Opera – Dr T.J. Walsh

The old saying 'ring up the curtain', comes from the theatre and means that when a bell is rung the stage curtains are opened. For Dr Thomas J. Walsh, 'the curtain was rung up' on 21 October 1951, when the first Wexford Festival of Opera and the Arts was born on the stage of the Theatre Royal, Wexford.

This venerable 'old lady' of High Street witnessed many changes since the doors of the theatre first opened in 1832. Visiting touring opera companies such as Carl Rosa, Moody and Manners, and Bowyer and Westwood played the Theatre Royal, presenting *Maritana*, *Bohemian Girl*, *Lily of Killarney*, *Rose of Castille*, *Il Trovatore*, and many other operatic works. The theatre also served as a cinema following the removal of the galleries and boxes, and then during the war years it gradually began to fall into disrepair and decay. At one point the theatre was used to store furniture, but a new day dawned for the Theatre Royal with the Wexford Festival of Opera and the Arts.

Thomas J. Walsh was born in 1911 in Wexford town, oldest son of John and Margaret Walsh. A younger brother, John, became a famous actor and television star – he played the role of Uncle James in the BBC's *The Forsyth Saga*. His only sister, Nellie Walsh, was the celebrated ballad singer, folk-song collector, and long-time compiler of the 'Songs and Cookery' pages for *Ireland's Own*. The Walshes were an extremely talented and artistic family who were deeply involved in the choral and theatrical life of their small provincial town. Tom Walsh always had an interest in music and singing, and took his first piano lessons with Miss Mary Codd, the church organist. He soon became a member of the Franciscan Church Choir, whose organist was Philip Pierce, owner of the Pierce Agricultural Machinery firm in Wexford. Later in life Tom Walsh had vocal training from the famous singing teacher and musician Maestro Viani in Dublin in 1930.

At this time the Walsh family were in the bar and grocery trade in the John Street area of Wexford town. Young Tom was pursuing his dream of studying medicine at UCD when tragedy struck: his father, John Walsh, died. Having completed the first year of his studies, Tom Walsh returned to Wexford, where he was offered his father's job with Daly's of Cork. While in Cork, Tom attended operatic productions at the Cork Opera House.

On his return to Wexford, with the encouragement of other music enthusiasts, he resurrected the old Wexford Operatic Society, renamed the Wexford Musical Society. Tom Walsh was in his element as producer: he used a cyclorama, and replaced the painted back-cloth cut-outs and moveable scenery pieces, giving a spacious effect to the productions.

Gilbert and Sullivan operas and musicals were the order of the day, until the early years of the Second World War caused the society's early demise. In the meantime Tom's younger brother John found himself unemployed – war shortages made salesmen redundant. He joined forces with Tom, and the Wexford Theatre Guild was born. Local and professional 'leads' came to the fore. Producing cavalcades, one-act plays and scenes from well-known operas, gave Tom Walsh the hands-on experience he needed for the great adventure that lay ahead. Tom Walsh returned to his medical studies and qualified as a doctor at Dublin University in 1944 and then set up and practiced in Wexford between 1944 and 1955. From 1955 to 1977 he was employed as an anaesthetist by Wexford County Hospital. During this time Dr Walsh married Eva Cousins, who was extremely talented musically and artistically, and a wonderful pianist. In 1950, Dr Tom, as he was affectionately known, set up the Opera Study Circle in Wexford, which met at White's Hotel for evenings of listening to gramophone records and occasional lectures. For its inaugural meeting, Dr Tom invited Sir Compton Mackenzie, then editor of *The Gramophone* magazine, to give a lecture to the society. At the close of the evening, Sir Compton suggested to Dr Walsh that 'live on-stage' opera was not beyond the bounds of possibility and much better than listening to recordings of opera. This idea appealed to Walsh very much.

With their shared love of opera uniting them, a hotelier, a postman and three medical doctors decided to join forces. Dr Tom's experience and expertise made him the obvious choice for Artistic Director, and together they made the Wexford Festival of Opera and the Arts a reality. The Theatre Royal was cleaned up, and a veritable army of volunteer workers was recruited, with local craftsmen building the stage scenery and fitting up the antiquated lighting board. Once the advertising was done, the tickets had gone on sale, rehearsals were well in hand, the visiting principal stars had been contracted, a local chorus made up from church choirs, and a male voice choir and other musical societies had been involved, it was almost time to 'ring up the curtain'. Dr Walsh selected Balfe's *Rose of Castille* because it was one of the composer's lesser performed works, and because as a youth Balfe had spent some time in Wexford. With the house-lights dimmed, Dermot O'Hara,

Dr T.J. Walsh, founder of the Wexford Festival
of Music and the Arts.

conductor of the Radio Eireann Orchestra, made his entrance into the hushed
auditorium. Once his baton was raised the overture played, and the very first voice
heard across the foot-lights was the rich contralto Nellie Walsh, singing the role of
Louisa, an innkeeper. The Wexford Festival of Opera and the Arts had begun.

Over the next fifteen years, Dr T.J. Walsh and his Festival Council presented no
less than thirty operas, covering Italian, French, German, and two Irish composers
(Michael William Balfe and Charles Villiers Stanford). Singers made their operatic
debuts, and used Wexford Festival as a spring-board to other opera houses. One of
the most famous singers to come to Wexford was Mirella Freni. The production
of lesser-known operas brought impresarios to Wexford to view these works for
the first time in the pocket-sized theatre in High Street.

Dr Walsh and his Opera Festival became a major force in the operatic world
and were soon ranked with Bayreuth, Salzburg; Glyndeborne and Aldeburgh
Festivals. Recitals were an integral part of the festival, with luminaries like pianists Julius Katchen, Paul Badura-Skoda, Rosalyn Tureck, and woodwind players
Leon Goosens and Elaine Shaffer, and violinist Alfredo Campoli and guitarist
Andres Segovia. Orchestras like the BBC Symphony and the Halle with Sir John
Barbirolli also performed at the festival. In those halcyon years, Wexford Festival
admission prices for recitals ranged from 10/6; 7/6 and 5/- with admission of 5/-
for the operatic dress rehearsals.

Many honours were bestowed on Dr Walsh, including an honorary Ph.D. and
D.Litt. from UCD, and a Fellowship of the Royal Historical Society. He was also
a Knight of Malta and a Freeman of the Town of Wexford. In addition to this, Dr

Walsh left his mark in the literary world with a series of scholarly publications and books on the history of opera. He probably did not imagine that the Festival of Opera and the Arts that he started in 1951 would still exist fifty-five seasons later, and be preparing to undergo a complete make-over. Dr T.J. Walsh died in November 1988, just two weeks before his seventy-seventh birthday. He is buried on the outskirts of Wexford in Barntown.

22

Seamus Ennis – Collector, Folklorist and Irish Piper

A piper in the street today,
Set up, and tuned, and started to play,
And away, away, away on the tide
Of his music we started; on every side.

The opening words of Seamus O'Sullivan's poem 'the Piper' are a perfect description of Seamus Ennis, the renowned uilleann piper, in every sense. He had that magical quality and the ability to gather an audience to listen and watch in awe as his very long, thin fingers encouraged musical notes to stream from the chanter of his uilleann pipes – tunes that were ornamented with rolls, pops, crans and grace notes, underscored by his drones and regulator chordal effects. He was an absolute genius to whom it was no bother to sit and play an endless catalogue of tunes interlaced with stories and folklore in Irish, English, and Scots Gaelic. Seamus Ennis was truly a Pied Piper who wove a fine spell over any audience, mesmerised by this Prince of Pipers.

Seamus Ennis was born in Jamestown in Finglas – a rural part of County Dublin at that time – on 5 May 1919. He was one of six children born to James Ennis and Mary Josephine McCabe who hailed from County Monaghan. His father was a civil servant and came from the Naul in County Dublin. Regarding his music, Seamus Ennis didn't 'take it off the wind', for his father was a multi-instrumentalist who played the uilleann pipes, among many other instruments, and was also a champion Irish dancer.

The young Ennis attended school at the Holy Faith Convent in Glasnevin and at Belvedere College. He also attended all-Irish schools at Scoil Cholm Cille and Coláiste Mhuire. The family regularly visited the Connemara Gaeltacht, where they stayed near Rosmuc, where Pearse had his Irish school. His father was a

Seamus Ennis, the Finglas piper who excelled at playing the uilleann pipes and tin whistle.

lover of all things Irish and gave the young Ennis a good grounding in the Irish language, which he developed and used to the full. This proficiency in the Irish language proved a great asset in later years, especially in his major work of collecting folk songs and tunes for the Radio Eireann and BBC sound archives. Seamus had this wonderful ability to converse in the regional Gaelic dialects with people in Connemara, Donegal, Kerry and even in Gaelic-speaking areas of Scotland. As a child Seamus remembered going to sleep to the sound of his father's pipes and was always very much aware of the traditional melodies.

Ennis sat an examination for the post of Employment Exchange Clerk and missed being called by one place. Soon after, he met Colm O'Lochlainn, a family friend, who was a publisher and owner of a printing firm (called At the Sign of the Three Candles) in Fleet Street, Dublin. Colm offered Seamus a job, and he worked at the printing firm from 1938 to 1942 becoming very adept at musical transcription for the printing of music books. It was Colm O'Lochlainn's firm that printed the two wonderful volumes of *Irish Street Ballads*. Seamus sang with the Irish language choir An Claisceadal, which was directed by O'Loughlainn and through this Ennis was introduced to Professor Seamus O'Duilearga of the Irish Folklore Commission.

Ennis played a very important role as a collector and folklorist, gathering music, song, and story throughout Ireland and Great Britain.

Soon, Ennis was offered a job with the Folklore Commission, where he worked from 1942 until 1947, moving on to Radio Eireann as Outside Broadcast Officer where he served until 1951. From 1951 Seamus Ennis began collecting for the BBC as part of a team led by Brian George. This work of collecting music, song, story, and folklore took Seamus to London, which became the base for his many journeys across Ireland, England, Scotland and Wales.

The resulting work was broadcast in a Sunday morning folk programme entitled 'As I Roved Out', which ran for nine years. The listenership was massive and the programme became a firm favourite with many people. Seamus Ennis' great gift for storytelling and for recounting meetings, happenings and events made him the ideal presenter of such a programme. All the while, the BBC was building up a massive and comprehensive store of the very best of the folk genre.

Seamus married Margaret Glynn in 1952, while living in London, and they had two children: Catherine and Christopher. His daughter is the renowned and internationally known organist Catherine Ennis. Catherine has demonstrated a great interest in the music her father played, especially in some recordings made with uilleann piper Liam O'Flynn, including the beautiful arrangement of the slow-air 'Easter Snow', a great favourite of her father's.

Seamus Ennis was a very tall, handsome man, with great independence and a gift for communication, who was courteous and knowledgeable, and well-versed in all things Gaelic. He has left many recordings, including 'The Return from Fingal' and the music- and story-cassette, 'The King of Ireland's Son' which will serve as testimony to his piping skills. An uilleann pipes tutor book was assembled and produced posthumously from his notes by Wilbert Garvin and Robbie Hannan, and published by Na Piobáirí Uilleann at Henrietta Street, Dublin.

Throughout his life, Seamus was a full-time collector of music, song, and story, with his two finest sources being Colm O'Caodháin, who contributed over 200 items of song, music and lore, while Elizabeth (Bess) Cronin from Baile Bhúirne in County Cork also made a great contribution from her store of songs 'ar an sean-nos'. This huge collection is stored in the Department of Irish Folklore at the National University of Ireland, Dublin, and is made up of music notation, manuscripts, texts, and sound recordings. It is a veritable treasure trove of traditional folklore, music and song.

Seamus Ennis' piping style greatly influenced the younger generation of Irish pipers, including Liam O'Flynn and Peter Browne, both of whom adopted some of Ennis' piping techniques and characteristics in their own playing. The final years of Seamus Ennis' life were plagued by ill health. He lived at the Naul, close to where he was born, and where his father's people were from. Seamus Ennis died in 1982 leaving a gap in the world of all things traditional and Gaelic. Long may the sounds of this wonderful exponent of the uilleann pipes be heard and marvelled at.

23.

Sean Maguire – Master Belfast Fiddler

Irish fiddler Sean Maguire had a distinctive sound from the moment his bow struck the strings, sounding the opening chord, to the final stroke of the bow that would bring another electrifying performance to a close. Maybe it was not the purist's idea of traditional fiddling, but the virtuoso playing, bowing, and fingering of Sean Maguire could not be ignored. Many tried to emulate the Belfast man's playing and some performers were even moderately successful, yet, none could scale the musical heights achieved by the fiddle maestro.

Sean Maguire was born in Belfast, son of Johnny (Jack) Maguire of Callanagh, Kilcogy, County Cavan. His father played the piccolo, flute and tin whistle. He had inherited his music from his own father, so music was in the blood. Jack Maguire moved to Belfast in 1918, and while his main interest was the tin whistle, he played piccolo in several céili bands.

Jack encouraged his son, Sean, to play the fiddle and from an early age he studied violin with Dr George Vincent. Following Dr Vincent's death, Sean's studies continued with Madam Mai Nesbitt, who made Sean perfect his bow-hand and technique through rigorous practice for months on end. By this time the youthful Maguire was working as an apprentice machinist, which curtailed his opportunity to practice and to play. His classical training took him through all the disciplines, from playing scales, arpeggios, sight reading, and the art of double-stopping to finger positions in the upper register of his instrument.

Well-prepared and grounded in the classical style, Sean was encouraged by his father to take up playing traditional Irish music, and he did so with great success. Jigs, reels and hornpipes just flowed from his magic bow with all kinds of delightful variations and ornamentations, bringing a fresh approach to many tunes. His playing and interpretation of the reel 'The Mason's Apron' has become synonymous with his name, for its tone and colour variations throughout the different eight-bar strains.

A youthful Sean Maguire as he appeared on an album cover.

Sean did his first broadcast when he was fifteen years of age on BBC Overseas Radio, and following his Oireachtas win in 1949 he began broadcasting from Radio Eireann on a regular basis. Sean became a professional musician at that time and continued to work as one for forty years. He also played the uilleann pipes, concert flute, tin whistle, guitar, and piano. He included some tracks on the uilleann pipes on his many recordings, playing his Belfast hand-made set of pipes, made by Frank McFadden. Together with his father Sean played with the Malachy Sweeney Céili Band and with Johnny Pickering's Céili Band before setting up his own band, with which he toured England and made several recordings.

It was with the Gael-Linn Cabaret that Sean toured America and Canada in the company of harper Kathleen Watkins, dancer Gráinne McCormack, singers Liam Devally, Mícheál ÓConaill, Breandán ÓDubhaill, Deirdre Ní Fhloinn, pianist Eilí Ní Mharcaigh and fear 'a-ti Diarmuid ÓBroin. They received critical acclaim for their cabaret-style Irish programme right across the United States. Their work was issued on an LP by Gael-Linn in the sixties, and Sean Maguire made several recordings for Gael-Linn, including one LP of mainly set-dances and some hornpipes. His early 78rpm records were issued mainly on the Decca green label, and later recordings were for HMV.

Sean used piano accompaniment to great advantage on his recordings and some of his pianists included Eileen Lane, Josephine Keegan, Eileen Markey, and in later years Pat McCabe. I was fortunate enough to act as accompanist for him on numerous occasions, which was always an exhilarating experience. On other

American tours he was a guest on the famous Ed Sullivan and Arthur Godfrey shows, enthralling millions of viewers with his brilliant playing. Carnegie Hall was another platform for Sean, where he made several appearances.

The Wurlitzer trust in New York are the custodians of Stradivarius and Guarnerius violins, which can be played by invitation only, and Sean Maguire was listed as one of their expert professional violinists. His name is included in the guest book with the names of other famous violinists like Fritz Kreisler and Yehudi Menuhin. Some regard Maguire's fiddling falling outside what can be regarded as traditional music, while others regard it as the finest fiddling.

What must be regarded as one of his finest recordings is that made with the Four Star Quartet. For this recording Sean invited Willie Joe Power, banjo-mandolinist extraordinaire; Eileen Lane, his favourite piano accompanist; and Sean Cotter, orchestral bassist, to join him in a vibrant selection of jigs, reels, hornpipes and set dances. Sean's mesmerizing rendition of 'The Mason's Apron', 'Mathematician' and his elegant 'Kilkenny Races' rate as some of his finest work, in my opinion. If it is ever released again on CD it is well worth having in any collection of traditional music.

In later years Sean suffered from a severe and debilitating illness but recovered sufficiently to be able to recover his speech, and to keep on giving concerts throughout Ireland. Teaching young violinists was a great joy for him, especially when they became as proficient as Maeve O'Hare, one of his star pupils. He also formed a small fiddle orchestra with some of his students, with one member even travelling all the way from Wexford to take part – such was the dedication Maguire inspired and which he himself gave to his students. Early in 2006 Sean had a severe stroke, which eventually resulted in his death at Easter 2006, much to the regret of his wife and family, and a multitude of friends and admirers throughout Ireland.

Brendan Breathnach, the music collector and musician, described Sean Maguire as 'gifted with amazing powers of execution able to toss off reel after reel in riotous variations.' Sean Maguire described his mixed style of classical and Scottish as 'progressive traditional'. Often frowned-upon by traditionalists, Sean Maguire was nevertheless one of a kind and inimitable.

24.

Dermot Troy – Shine Through My Dreams

Ireland has produced many fine male singers over the years: John McCormack, James Johnston, Joseph McLaughlin, Louis Browne, Austin Gaffney, Frank Patterson, Brendan O'Dowda, Martin Dempsey, and Brendan Cavanagh, for example. Today we also have fine singing from Finbarr Wright, Anthony Kearns, Ronan Tynan and, of course, the Celtic Tenors. One star, alas, passed from our midst at a very young age, when the world of opera was at his feet: Dermot Troy died at the age of only thirty-five.

Dermot was born in Tinahely, Wicklow on 31 July, 1927. On finishing school at CBS, Synge Street, Dublin, he took off for England where he joined the RAF at the age of eighteen. He served with the men in their flying machines for three and a half years before returning to Ireland because of family commitments. Following a singing appearance at a concert in Dublin, it was suggested to young Dermot that he take singing lessons with Professor Michael O'Higgins, the renowned singing teacher. Among Professor O'Higgins' students were Gerald Duffy, Austin Gaffney, Rosemary McDonald and Eithne McGrath, who was later to become Dermot's wife. As a member of a choral group from Professor O'Higgins' academy, Troy helped win the Culwick Cup at the Feis Ceoil in 1950.

In 1952, the *Sunday Independent* ran a competition in connection with the film *The Great Caruso*, featuring Mario Lanza, and Dermot Troy won it, with Corkman Michael Murphy taking second place. The next step for Troy was to compete in England. When he got there it transpired that the competition was not confined to tenors, and the eventual winner was a baritone, with Dermot taking second place. In the audience on the final night was the chief vocal coach of Glynebourne Opera, Jani Strasser, who immediately invited Dermot Troy to participate in the forthcoming Glynebourne Season as a member of the chorus. Strasser also offered Dermot the opportunity to understudy several roles.

Dermot Troy, pictured
when he was an
emerging young
Irish tenor who won
great acclaim in the
operatic world.

After leaving Glynebourne, Dermot joined the Royal Opera House to play
small roles and at the same time continue his vocal studies with Dino Borgioli. It
was not long before he was noticed by one of England's most distinguished music
critics, Ernest Newman. Newman wrote glowing reviews of Dermot's interpretation of the sailor in the revival of Berlioz's, *Les Troyens*, and praised him for the
beauty of his tone when singing the part of David in *Die Meistersinger*. Coming
from a critic of Newman's stature, this was high praise indeed. Later, Newman
also singled Dermot out for his performance as the chaplain in *The Carmelites*, by
Poulenc.

In 1954, Dermot married Eithne McGrath, another former pupil of Michael
O'Higgins', and three years later the Opera House in Mannheim, Germany,
offered to make Dermot their leading lyric tenor – with great success. Very
soon he was in great demand in all the leading opera houses in Germany. Guest
appearances followed in Frankfurt, Munich, Düsseldorf, Stuttgart, and many
other opera houses, where he played to great acclaim in Rossini's, *The Barber
of Seville*, *La Cenerentola*, and in Mozart's, *Così fan tutte*, *The Magic Flute* and *Don
Giovanni*.

It was while making a guest appearance at the Hamburg State Opera, where he performed in *Il Seraglio* – going on stage without any preliminary rehearsals – that the General Manager of the Opera House, composer Rolf Liebermann, offered Dermot a three year contract. This was a great honour, and a sure sign that the young Irish tenor had 'arrived'. Hamburg rated, with Munich and Berlin, as one of the major opera houses in Germany.

Even though Dermot Troy had a very short life, his operatic career was astonishing, filled with many lyric roles that endeared him to his audiences. He was regarded as one of the leading Mozartian tenors on the continent and his rendition of 'Dies Bildnis ist bezaubernd schön' from *The Magic Flute* was truly unique. When Troy performed as Don Ottavio in *Don Giovanni* with Joan Sutherland in the 1958 Dublin Grand Opera Season, the *Irish Times* music critic Charles Acton commented, 'as this is his first major role at home it was all the more pleasing. 'Il mio tesoro' was beautifully sung'.

His operatic roles covered a wide range, from Tamino in *The Magic Flute*, Don Ottavio in *Don Giovanni*, Lenski in *Eugen Onegin*, Vasak in *The Bartered Bride*, the helmsman in *The Flying Dutchman*, Don Riccardo in *The Triumph of Love*, to Cassio in *Othello*. This really was an extensive repertoire for such a young tenor and made great vocal and physical demands on the singer. His operatic performances in Haydn's *Untreue lohnt sich nicht (L'infedeltà delusa)* were televised twice after his death.

He sang roles in the Royal Opera House, Covent Garden, Glynbourne Opera House, as well as the main German opera houses, in the company of such singers as Mattiwilda Dobbs, Maria Callas, Joan Sutherland, Adele Leigh, Magda Lászlò, Pilar Lorengar, Gisela Litz, Joan Carlisle and Ireland's Veronica Dunne. He also performed with male singers Frederick Dalberg, James Johnston, Hermann Prey, Thomas Tipton and the Irish bass, David Kelly.

Possibly one of the highlights of Dermot Troy's career was the personal invitation from soprano Elisabeth Schwarzkopf to sing the role of the Italian singer in Richard Strauss' *Capriccio*, which was recorded by HMV in Salzburg. Madam Schwarzkopf remarked that his voice was the one she had been waiting for. Also taking part in this recording were Dieter Fischer-Dieskau, Hans Hotter and Anna Moffo – exalted company indeed for our Irish tenor.

Those who worked with Dermot Troy knew and admired him for his modesty, sincerity, generosity and above all for his wit and infectious laughter, and described him as resembling John McCormack in looks and stature.

Following a heart attack in June 1961, Dermot spent weeks recuperating and then resumed his singing in Hamburg in 1962, where he died on 6 September of that year. He was mourned by his colleagues in the opera houses of Germany and Britain, as well as by all those who admired him in Ireland. Most of his recordings are now unavailable, which is a great pity. On the odd occasion when one of these recordings is broadcast people stop, listen, admire his voice and try, usually unsuccessfully, to identify his voice.

In 1960 Dermot O'Hara, conductor of the Radio Eireann Light Orchestra, made a series of recordings with Dermot Troy. These recordings, entitled *Songs to Remember* and featuring fourteen favourite songs in the delightful lyric tenor voice of Dermot Troy, were issued by RTE on a vinyl record.

25

Seán Ó Riada – from Classical to Folk

When Seán Ó Riada's name is mentioned in music circles his film score for George Morrison's *Mise Éire* inevitably comes up. He created wonderful musical effects by carefully using the orchestra and he used many of our best-loved traditional airs in creative ways. The main theme was 'Róisín Dubh', in which Ireland is represented as the Dark Rose, one of its many allegorical names. The sean-nós version of 'Sliabh na mBan', together with 'Boolavogue', 'Who Fears to Speak of Ninety-Eight', and 'The Croppy Boy' were also adapted by Ó Riada to highlight various important moments in Ireland's struggle for freedom. The flickering black and white footage so carefully restored and edited by George Morrison was further enhanced by Ó Riada's wonderful score. The foremost music critic of the day, Charles Acton, went on to say that "Mise Éire' proves that Ireland has a composer of film-music as good as anyone in the world. In this film, Seán Ó Riada seems to have Mozart's knack of putting exactly the right notes in exactly the right places – no more, no less – and Gustav Mahler's ability to use strange rich colours with a sparse austerity'. This was wonderful praise indeed for a composer who had struggled to make a name for himself in Ireland.

Born in 1931 in Cork, John Reidy and his sister Louise were the only surviving children of Sean and Julia Reidy. His father, a native of Kilmihil, County Clare, was a Garda Sergeant stationed in Adare, County Limerick, where John Reidy grew up. His mother was Julia Creedon, from Kilnamartra in the Barony of West Muskerry, County Cork, and came from a musical background, as did his father. He received his first music lessons at the age of seven from Granville Metcalfe, a violin teacher who came out to Adare from Limerick City once a week to give lessons in the area. A year later the young Reidy went on to learn the piano, with theory, counterpoint and harmony, from Professor Van de Veld, and at the age of ten he joined the Limerick Music Club where he performed until he left for boarding school at Farranferris in 1943.

In 1948 John Reidy entered University College Cork by scholarship to read for an Arts degree. Latin, Greek, and Irish were his main subjects but towards the end of his first year he decided to change to music full time. He studied under Professor Aloys Fleischmann Senior, who felt that Reidy was the most gifted young man in the music department. One of Reidy's first arrangements was a setting of the air 'Slán le Máigh', a song in praise of his own place. A later skilful orchestral scoring of Schumann's piano work 'Papillon' for the Cork Ballet Company was widely acclaimed. John Reidy obtained a Bachelors Degree in Music with Honours in 1952. His final musical work was examined by Sir Arnold Bax, the English composer.

During his studies at university he played be-bop jazz and was often to be found belting out intricate piano improvisations with Cork's leading jazz men, such as Bobby Lambe, Johnny Cagney, and the Billy Browne Combo. These musicians thought very highly of the young student and predicted a promising career in jazz music for him. Reidy enjoyed the smokey atmosphere of Cork's jazz clubs but his sole ambition in life, by his own admission, was to be a composer – and a good one.

Following his marriage to Ruth Coghlan in 1953, he landed the job of Assistant Music Director at Radio Eireann at the GPO in Henry Street, Dublin. The tedious paperwork involved did not appeal to John Reidy, as he said himself: 'I have not composed any music since I took this position'. So at twenty-four years of age he decided to leave his £800-a-year civil service position and head to Paris, which he believed to be the centre of the artistic world. Reidy had excellent French and this was his final bid for freedom and for time to devote himself to composition. It was not to be, however – he lived almost in poverty with very little opportunity to compose. French Radio broadcast one programme featuring his music. John Reidy returned to Ireland never to live abroad again. He said 'I'd rather be breaking stones in Ireland than be the richest man living in Europe'.

At this time his most prolific period of composition and orchestral and choral arranging began, with original works for the National Symphony Orchestra as well as the Radio Eireann Singers and Light Orchestra. His base in Dublin and his job as music director at the Abbey Theatre gave him the time to work on these compositions. Reidy discovered the serialism of Arnold Schoenberg and his technique of atonality, and this led to one of Reidy's earliest compositions, 'Nomos No.1'. It was based on the words 'Hercules Dux Ferrariae'. Hercules was the renowned patron of music and the arts and was Duke of Ferrara. It was composed for string orchestra and based on the musical notes D, F, E, D, C, D, C, D, giving eight sections each, based on one of these musical notes. It is available on record as played by the string section of the London Philharmonic Orchestra conducted

The untimely death of
Ó Riada deprived Irish
music of a composer
who would have had
much more to offer.

by Carlo Franci. As a tribute to his music professor, Aloys G. Fleischmann, Reidy
set four poems by the German poet Johann Christian Friedrich Holderlin to
music in 1964. Along with these compositions, recorded by Bernadette Greevy,
one can also find poems by Thomas Kinsella, John Montague, Seamus Heaney
and the French poet, painter, and founder member of the Dada movement Hans
Arp, all accompanied beautifully on the piano by Veronica McSwiney. Acclaimed
by critics for his European influences and mastery of the orchestra, Reidy seemed
to be the composer Ireland had been waiting for.

It was in 1959 that John Reidy was commissioned by Gael-Linn to write the
score for *Mise Eire,* a documentary assembled by George Morrison. It mainly featured events surrounding the founding of the Irish Free State and because it was
released so close to the fiftieth anniversary of the 1916 Rising it was influential in
the establishment of an Irish cultural identity. When he heard the music the poet
Thomas Kinsella, a friend of Reidy's, commented, 'He has wrung from his basic
theme, (Róisín Dubh), in full Mahlerian and Sibelian harmonies, every emo-
tional possibility. It is a monument to his talent that the results, while devastating

the audience for whom it was produced, remains a fine musical achievement'. The year 1960 brought 'Saoirse' another work by George Morrison, followed by 'An Tine Bheo' in 1966, compiled and directed by Louis Marcus. At the opening night of *Mise Eire* many of those who had participated in and survived the Rising at the GPO, including Eamonn DeValera and Sean T. O'Ceallaigh, were present.

Reidy now totally immersed himself in every aspect of Gaelic culture, including the language, tales of conquest, and sagas. The literature and poetry of Donal Corkery, Eoghan Ruadh O'Suilleabháin, Peadar O'Doirnín *et al.* became an integral part of his life. John Reidy had receded into the shadows and his 'new' persona – Seán Ó Riada – had emerged.

Seán Ó Riada began experimenting with traditional music and groupings of traditional instruments resulting in the group Ceoltóirí Chualann. As a folk orchestra they provided incidental music for Brian McMahon's play *The Honey Spike* at the Abbey Theatre. Ceoltóirí Chualann were an instant success, gaining a wide following even though they made very few concert appearances. They were known principally from their radio programmes 'Reachaireacht an Riadaigh' and 'Fleadh Cheoil an Raidio', and especially from their recordings for Gael-Linn and Ceirníní Cladaigh, 'Ó Riada sa Gaiety' in particular.

Seán played bodhrán with the group in the beginning, transferring to harpsichord at a later stage. He resigned from the Abbey Theatre in 1962 and moved to Corca Duibhne for a year, where he freelanced for RTE and wrote for *The Irish Times*. His appointment as Assistant Lecturer in music at University College Cork came in 1963, with a move by the family to An Draighean, Cúil Aodha. Ó Riada had found his niche, especially as Cúil Aodha was only ten miles from his mother's birthplace. He formed a local choir, Cóir Cúil Aodha, and wrote his first Irish Mass for them in 1965. Sean composed a second Mass for Glenstall Abbey in 1968, and a Requiem that was commissioned by the Irish government.

His lectures broadcast on Radio Eireann entitled 'Our Musical Heritage', which eventually appeared in book form, were of great interest to students of traditional music. In these lectures Seán's assessment of styles of sean-nós singing was enlightening, but his harsh treatment of some musical instruments used in traditional music and ceílí bands in particular drew caustic comments from some musicians.

Seán Ó Riada, together with John Kelly, Sean Keane, Paddy Moloney, Sean Potts, Michael Tubridy, Eamonn de Buitléar, Martin Fay, Peadar Mercier and singer Sean O'Sé, collectively known as Ceoltóirí Chualann, created a new style for this type of music. Many of these famous musicians carried on this revival initiated by Ó Riada.

Sean Ó Riada's funeral took place on a very rainy day in 1971. Ireland's foremost musicians, writers, poets, and friends carried his mortal remains, shoulder high like a chieftain, preceded by a lone war-piper, to his resting place at Cúil

Aodha. A nation's tears mingled with the falling rain as they bade farewell to a composer *agus fear usail* who had, in essence, returned the national folk music to the people.

26.

The Harp that Once...

The harp that once produced delightful melodies in the capable hands of harper Derek Bell fell silent on 17 October 2002 in Phoenix, Arizona, when Bell died. A routine surgical procedure from which he never recovered deprived the world of music of one of its most talented performers and characters. Derek Bell's passing has left a void not alone in the world of Irish traditional music but also in that of classical music, a genre for which he was trained.

Derek Fleetwood Bell was born on 21 October 1935 in Belfast to William Bell, a banker, and his wife Shelagh. As a two-year-old child Derek was misdiagnosed with an infant sight ailment and his parents were told that their son was going blind. He was, in fact, simply very short-sighted, and this was soon corrected with glasses. Derek's parents were advised to buy musical toys to develop the boy's sense of hearing (to compensate for the loss of his eyesight). This was the beginning of a life-long musical interest. Very soon Derek Bell graduated to playing on real musical instruments.

Derek's mother died when he was five years old, so his father brought him and his sister, Déirdre, up by himself. At the age of nine Derek began to take piano lessons, and he was soon regarded as a child prodigy. He composed his first piano concerto at the age of eleven and sent it to the BBC, requesting that it be played by the renowned violinist Yehudi Menuhin on the radio. The BBC were so impressed with the youth's audacity that they invited him into the broadcasting studio the following week to play one of his piano pieces. At the time, Derek Bell was in boarding school, so following 'lights out' he composed a few short piano pieces which he played the next week at the BBC. The BBC's musical panel was so impressed that Derek was offered a slot, becoming a regular performer on 'Children's Hour'.

Derek Bell was convinced that it was his destiny to be a musician – against his father's wishes, who thought that it was too precarious a means of earning a living. His father decided that if his son was good enough to obtain a scholarship that would pay for his training he could proceed. In the meantime, the fifteen-year-old had also become proficient on the oboe, which he played in the school orchestra. A year later the ambitious teenager won a composition scholarship to the Royal College of Music in London. His father was very impressed and built a home practice studio for his son. Derek Bell was on his way up at last.

Derek travelled to London, where he studied for the next few years before travelling to Colorado to study piano with Madam Rosina Lhévinne and to study harp with Artiss de Volt in Salzburg. As a soloist, Derek Bell had an impressive career and performed with great symphony orchestras like the Berlin, Moscow, Budapest, Pittsburg, Liverpool, London and the Irish National Symphony Orchestra in Dublin. This all happened when Derek was in his twenties and thirties. It was while serving as an oboist that Derek got the task of tuning the orchestral harps for concerts. He learned very quickly to bring the harps up to concert pitch by the use of a tuning fork. It was so much work that Derek eventually convinced himself to learn to play the harp himself. He went to Sheila Larchet-Cuthbert in Dublin for lessons and then to London to Gwendolen Mason.

In 1965 the head of BBC Music, Dr Boucher, appointed Derek Bell as Principal Harper with the orchestra, which brought with it extra money for also playing the oboe. As a classical musician of very high calibre, Derek Bell's tireless work was recognised by the Queen of England in her Official Honours List. Derek was invited to Buckingham Palace, where he was conferred with an MBE by Her Majesty. He was very pleased to be honoured and accepted his award with great pride. Over the years Derek had learned to play many musical instruments, including dulcimer, oboe d'amour, oboe cor anglais, harpsichord, organ, piano, keyboard, kurzweil synthesizer, timpán, Irish harp, and concert harp.

It was at a BBC St Patrick's Day Special that Derek Bell was invited to play harp with the top Irish folk group The Chieftains. When Paddy Moloney appeared at rehearsal with his uilleann pipes the entire orchestra crowded around to see the funny-looking instrument he was playing. On the night of the broadcast Derek Bell's harp-playing gave The Chieftains a completely new and wholly Irish sound. There was no going back. Paddy had been looking for the right person to play harp with his group, and he found him in Derek Bell. Audiences marvelled at this new sound from The Chieftains, as the mischievous-looking harper from Belfast basked in the limelight. The year was 1972.

Derek Bell had served as harper with the Northern Ireland BBC Orchestra, and was Professor of Harp and Irish Harp at the Belfast Academy of Music prior to taking his place with the globe-trotting Chieftains, a huge change indeed. On his many tours everyone wanted to meet Derek at the post-concert chats – he was extremely popular. Outrageously funny and witty, he enjoyed musical jokes and thought nothing of playing a few bars of the *Pink Panther* theme or a Scott

Joplin rag, while at the same time hopping up and down at the piano or seated at the harp. He played one piece of music in particular that was really magical. He was known by The Chieftains as 'The Professor', because of his quaint appearance, and was affectionately called 'Ding Dong Bell' by Paddy Moloney. Derek Bell's passing has deprived the musical world of a star performer. Fortunately, Derek left a considerable amount of recorded music for our continued enjoyment.

27.

Ruby Murray – Softly, Softly

Ruby Murray was born on 29 March, 1935, in Belfast. She was instantly recognizable by her hoarse singing voice, the result of a childhood operation, and it became her trademark.

Ruby began singing at an early age as a child singer in and around her home city. She was spotted by producer Richard Afton and made her television debut aged twelve. Her career came to a halt as stringent Irish laws regarding child performers held her back for two years.

She returned to school in Belfast until she was fourteen, and in 1954 travelled to London with Tommy Morgan's touring revue 'Mrs Mulligan's Hotel' where she was spotted once again by Richard Afton at the Metropolitan Theatre, Edgeware Road. He offered her a job as resident singer on the BBC's *Quite Contrary* here she replaced Joan Regan, who was leaving the show.

Ray Martin, recording manager and musical director for Columbia Records in England signed Ruby to the company and very soon released Ruby Murray's first record, 'Heartbeat'. Record sales were phenomenal and Ruby's record made the British Top 5 in 1954. This record was quickly followed by 'Softly, Softly', which reached the top of the hit parade and became a No.1 hit for Ruby in 1955. That same year she had five singles in the Top Twenty at the same time, a feat that was only surpassed by Madonna in the 1980s. Murray's hits included 'Happy Days and Lonely Nights', 'Let Me Go Lover', If Anyone Finds This, I Love You', 'Goodbye, Jimmy, Goodbye', and 'You Are My First Love'. This last song was voiced over by Ruby for the opening titles of the musical film 'It's Great to be Young'.

Ruby Murray's beautiful voice, which was described as 'sweet and tender and full of character', endeared her to millions of listeners and fans. She was regarded as 'the voice of Ireland' and became one of the most prominent performers in the UK and Ireland, eventually making her home in England.

'St Patrick's Day', an album that featured Ruby with many of Ireland's leading performers.

By this time Ruby had married Bernie Burgess, whom she met in 1957 while appearing in Blackpool. Bernie was a member of the vocal group the Jones Boys. They married in secret ten days after they met.

Ruby appeared in numerous shows and once under the direction of the famous Gordon Parry when she played a role in the comedy film *A Touch of the Sun*. The film starred comedian Frankie Howard and Dennis Price. Ruby Murray had an extremely busy career, especially in the mid-1950s. At this time she starred in her own television show and appeared at the famous London Palladium in a show called 'Painting the Town' with funny man Norman Wisdom. She also appeared in a Royal Command performance and afterwards was introduced to the Queen. Many British artists have toured the United Stated with only minimal success, but Ruby Murray had a very successful tour of the States. She also toured in Malta and North Africa. Her husband, Bernie Burgess, became her manager and they toured as a double act in the sixties.

In 1970 Ruby had some success with 'Change Your Mind', which prompted her to release an album with the same title. She included some contemporary

Ruby Murray in concert
with Brendan O'Dowda in a
St Patrick's Night Special.

songs such as 'Raindrops Keep Falling on My Head' and also revamped some
of her hit songs. Sadly, Ruby Murray's chart career was at an end. Her choice of
material and her shy image were probably just a little too sentimental for the less
innocent, more outgoing and outspoken 1960s. Flower Power and the Beatles
overshadowed performers like Ruby Murray.

Ruby remained a popular performer, and her LP recordings certainly were
not ignored, even into the 1970s. She performed on television and on the stage
with many of the top stars and had a memorable St Patrick's Night Irish Special
with County Louth singer Brendan O'Dowda. She never forgot her Irish roots,
recording such favourites as 'Teddy O'Neill', 'O'Malley's Tango', 'Macushla
Mine', 'Nora Malone' (Call me by Phone)', 'The Humour Is On Me Now', 'A
Pretty Irish Girl', and 'Connemara', both with Brendan O'Dowda. In 1989 Ruby
Murray's EMI Years release featured songs that she regularly sang in her stage act,
such as 'Mr Wonderful', 'Scarlet Ribbons' and 'It's the Irish in Me'.

The year 1990 saw Ruby Murray based in Torquay, Devon with her second
husband, the musical impresario Ray Lamar. She continued to perform regularly

even though in later years she came to be regarded as a nostalgia act and appeared in shows with other former stars of the fifties. Her devoted fans just really wanted to hear her sing her most famous hit songs. Songs like 'Knock on any Door', 'True Love', 'Little White Lies', 'My Little Corner of the World', and many, many more were given that special treatment by the husky-voiced singer from Belfast. Ruby Murray died on 18 December 1996. A play by Marie Jones about Ruby's life, entitled *Ruby*, opened at the Group Theatre in Belfast in April 2000.

28.

Frank Patterson – Ireland's Golden-Voiced Tenor

'It was seldom a voice of such splendid musical integrity was heard. The singer has such poise that his mind and heart were in very close contact with his singing.' These comments were made by Feis Ceoil adjudicator, Roy Hickman about young County Tipperary singer Frank Patterson when he competed in the category of tenor voice.

Patterson was born on 5 October 1938 in Clonmel, where his mother ran a small printing works. Frank was eventually apprenticed to the trade following his schooling. He enjoyed singing even as a young boy, and his musical career began when he was a boy soprano in his home town. His time at the printing works was short-lived, as he left that inky world and moved to Dublin for vocal training with Dr Hans Waldemar Rosen. Frank was twenty-four years of age. Following just two years of studying both singing and acting, the young tenor won all the major awards at Dublin's Feis Ceoil. This meant that Frank was then in great demand for classical recitals around Ireland, and he was particularly noted for his performances in oratorios.

In 1966, Frank Patterson toured America as soloist with a group of young Irish singers and dancers known as Feis Eireann. The musical director and pianist with the group was Eily O'Grady, a member of the well-known Dublin musical family. The inevitable happened: tenor and pianist fell in love on that tour and soon were married. This was the beginning of a long and harmonious marriage and a professional musical partnership. Following a four-month tour of the USA and Canada, Frank and Eily moved to London, where Frank could continue his vocal studies. Two years later, in 1968, Frank Patterson had the opportunity to study with French soprano Janine Micheau, which took the Pattersons to Paris. The four-year study was a daunting task for Frank and Eily, but concerts and radio performances helped to defray the costs of Frank's study.

While he lived in the USA, Frank Patterson had three television specials that aired coast-to-coast.

Both believed firmly in Frank's vocal talent, which consistently improved. A radio broadcast of songs by Purcell on the BBC brought Frank to the attention of Philips Record Company bosses. A contract was quickly drawn up with the record company and Frank recorded six albums in three years. This was a lot of work, but it was worth his while because it launched Frank Patterson's celebrated and distinguished career as a recording artist

After this, Frank recorded over forty albums in six different languages, rang-

ing from opera and oratorios to songs by composers like Handel, Beethoven,
Mozart, Purcell, Schubert and Berlioz. One of his albums included col-
laborations with Kiri Te Kanawa, José Carreras, Elly Amerling and Herman
Prey in a selection of arias by G.F. Handel and Hugo Wolf. Patterson often
crossed over from the world of classical music to popular, Broadway and Irish
music, which brought his lyric tenor voice to a wider audience. His increased
popularity was reflected in his record sales which brought him platinum, gold
and silver discs.

Concert recitals, radio and television broadcasts, and performances through-
out Europe as a soloist at the great musical festivals took Frank Patterson to
all the principal cities of Europe. He sang with the London Symphony, the
Academy of St Martin-in-the-Fields, the Liverpool Philharmonic, the Orchestre
de Paris, in Rome, in Basle and with the Irish National Symphony Orchestra.
In America, Frank sang in Carnegie Hall to a sold-out house. As part of the
American Centennial celebrations , Frank joined with American opera stars
Anna Moffo, Simon Estes and Robert Merrill in a rendition of Irving Berlin's,
'God Bless America' for a televised performance from St Patrick's Cathedral,
New York. Frank sang the American anthem many times in his concerts and it
was a favourite means of expressing his appreciation for his adopted country
and its people.

John Huston, director of *The Dead*, invited Frank to play the role of fic-
tional tenor Bartell D'Arcy, and this was followed by the role of Danny Boy
in Joel and Ethan Coehn's, *Miller's Crossing*. He also played the part of an Irish
tenor in the Neil Jordan movie *Michael Collins*, in which he sang Macushla.
Frank had his own television series, *Frank Patterson, For Your Pleasure* on RTE
from 1974 to 1984. Three American television specials, *Ireland's Golden Tenor
– Ireland in Song, Frank Patterson – Songs of Inspiration* and *God Bless America*
brought Frank critical acclaim throughout America. In 1982, President
Ronald Regan invited Frank and Eily to perform at the White House, and in
1995, together with their violinist son Eanan, they performed for President
Clinton.

The highlight of Frank Patterson's career was singing at the Papal Mass in the
Phoenix Park, Dublin, before 1.3 million people, and again when he sang for His
Holiness during the 1996 visit of Pope John Paul II to America. Frank Patterson
received many awards for his services to music and the arts, including Knight
of St Gregory, Knight of Malta, Knight Commander of the Holy Sepulchre
of Jerusalem, an Honorary Doctor of Music from Salve Regina University in
Newport, Rhode Island, and an Honorary Doctor of Fine Arts from Manhattan
College of New York. Both Frank and Eily were awarded the Gold Medal of the
Eire Society of Boston. The man from Clonmel who conquered the world of
music is honoured in his native town with a magnificent bronze life-sized sculpture by Jerry McKenna from Texas. The inscription on the pedestal states:

This sculpture is a tribute to Ireland's Ambassador of Song who brought the joy of classical and popular music as well as Irish culture into the hearts of millions throughout the world.

Following a brief illness Frank Patterson died on 10 June 2000.

29.

Luke Kelly – Ballad Singer and Dubliner

In 2004, Ireland commemorated the centenary of the birth of Monaghan poet Patrick Kavanagh and the twentieth anniversary of the death of Dublin singer Luke Kelly, who died at the early age of forty-four in 1984. The two men are inextricably linked by the poet's 'On Raglan Road', and the singer's definitive rendition to the air of 'Fáinne Geal an Lae'. Folk singer Luke Kelly was born on 17 November 1940 into a Dublin working-class family living on Sheriff Street, a short distance from bustling O'Connell Street. His Scottish grandmother, a McDonald, lived with the Kellys until her death in 1953.

Luke's father worked in Jacob's biscuit factory all his life and was an ardent soccer fan, and both Luke and his brother Paddy played hurling, Gaelic football, and soccer. The Kelly brothers attended O'Connell Schools where they received their formal education from the Christian Brothers. With north inner city redevelopment in 1953, the family were relocated to Whitehall, then a suburb of Dublin city. Luke was twelve years old at the time, and a year later left school to do odd-jobbing around the city, eventually leaving for England in 1958. It was here that he teamed up with his brother Paddy to do steel-fixing on a building site in Wolverhampton. Luke was sacked when he asked for more money, and later oil barrel cleaning and working as a vacuum cleaner salesman took Luke all over England.

While in the north of England, Luke visited a folk-club in Newcastle where he listened to the many and varied folk-songs and ballads from the north of England and Scotland. He was smitten with what he heard and very soon acquired a five-string banjo that became synonymous with his name and style of singing. In Leeds, he brought his banjo to sessions in McReady's pub, and his store of songs began to grow. He was also a constant visitor to the Communist Party headquarters in Leeds.

Luke Kelly pictured with singing idol
Tom Jones and *Dubliner* Ciarán Burke.

England was in the midst of a folk revival and at the centre of it was Ewan
McColl, who penned such classics as 'The Shoal of Herring', 'Dirty Ol' Town',
and many other fine ballads that Kelly soon made his own. Luke had found his
niche as he took up busking, singing his way from city to city and folk club to
folk club. He was on his way.

On a trip home to Ireland, he attended a Fleadh Cheoil in Milltown Malbay,
where his singing and music brought him much acclaim. As well as folk music
and ballads, Luke listened to the recordings of Woodie Guthrie and Pete Seeger
and perfected his own style and developed faultless diction. He also developed his
political convictions, which he held throughout his life.

Kelly returned to and lived in Birmingham, where he made many friends,
including Ned Stapleton, who taught Luke to sing 'The Rocky Road to Dublin'.
At this point, Luke took up the game of golf with a passion – he played on one
of Birmingham's municipal courses. He became involved in the Jug o' Punch folk
club run by another famous folk singer, Ian Campbell, and it was here that Luke
befriended Dominick Behan, brother of Brendan, and together they performed
in folk clubs and Irish pubs from London to Glasgow. It was during those times
that Luke met street singer Margaret Barry and musicians Seamus Ennis, Roger
Sherlock, Mairtín Burns, and Bobby Casey. He was a regular visitor to Ewan
McColl and Peggy Seeger's Singers Club in London.

The ballad boom had begun in Dublin in 1961, with sessions in the Abbey
Tavern in Howth, the Hollybrook in Clontarf, the International Bar, and the
Grafton Cinema, so it was time for Luke to return to his native Dublin, and 1962
saw Luke singing in O'Donoghue's with Ronnie Drew, Barney McKenna, the
Furey Family, John Keenan, Sean Og McKenna, and Johnny Moynihan. John
Molloy, the actor, organised a 'Ballad Tour of Ireland' in the Hibernian Hotel,
where Luke joined the Ronnie Drew Ballad Group. The success of this show
brought the group to the Abbey Tavern, the Royal Marine and the Embankment,
Tallaght. Soon the group were joined by Ciarán Bourke and John Sheehan, and
changed their name to the Dubliners. Success followed.

In 1964, Luke Kelly left the Dubliners, returned to London and became involved with Ewan McColl's The Critics, formed to explore folk traditions and help young singers. At this time, Luke married Deirdre O'Connell, founder of the Focus Theatre.

In 1966, Luke returned to his native city and rejoined The Dubliners. They recorded an album in Cecil Sharpe House, London, and played the Cambridge Folk Festival. A concert in the National Stadium, Dublin, resulted in Luke meeting Pete Seeger, who was a special guest and one of his heroes. Top Twenty hits included 'Seven Drunken Nights' and 'Black Velvet Band', an appearance on the Ed Sullivan Show in 1968, and a tour of New Zealand and Australia that brought world-wide recognition to Luke Kelly and the Dubliners.

Luke also took to the stage as King Herod in a production of *Jesus Christ Superstar*, and performed with the Dubliners in 1972 in *Richard's Cork Leg*, based on some of Brendan Behan's incomplete works. Two of Luke's greatest performances came as a result of an alliance with Derry-born musician and composer Phil Coulter, who composed and produced 'The Town I Loved So Well' and the poignant and moving 'Scorn Not His Simplicity'. During a concert in the Cork Opera House on 30 June 1980 Luke Kelly collapsed on stage with a brain tumour. A lengthy operation followed, and there seemed to be every hope for a full recovery. Four years later, in 1984, Luke collapsed again while on a tour of Switzerland. He died in hospital on 30 January of that year. Years later, following a proposal from Tony Gregory, Dublin City Council named a new bridge over the Tolka River in memory of Luke Kelly, and a statue to honour this great Dublin balladeer is being planned.

30

Comhaltas Ceoltóirí Eireann – Custodians of our National Folk Music

In past times the arts of traditional music, song and dance were mainly practised within rural households with house dances and musical evenings. With the day's work over, the supper eaten, the rosary recited, the flagged floor in the kitchen swept clean, and the flames of the open fire leaping up the chimney, the lamps were lit and the door was opened wide with a *céad míle fáilte* to all who crossed the threshold. Young and old gathered in anticipation of the evening's entertainment. Fiddles tuned, bows rosined, flutes blown and pipes pitched, all ready for the profusion of jigs, reels, hornpipes and airs of the 'big songs' to be performed. Many an enjoyable evening was had as the moon paled and the morning sky was reddened by the rising sun of the new day before the music ceased. Festive times, weddings, christenings, American wakes and Christmas all brought out the music, song, dance and epic stories of our ancient heroes and heroines. However, it was a 'new dawn' that brought the celebration of such festivities to and end – the Dance Hall Act of 1939. The death knell sounded for the house dances and sessions, as they were relegated to a fading past. The traditional practitioners were cast out, as their brand of music did not appeal to the new mood created by the dance halls and 'boogie woogie'.

In an effort to counteract this threat and to preserve our native music, representatives of the Piper's Club of Thomas Street, Dublin, met with traditional music enthusiasts from Mullingar, Westmeath, with a view to doing something positive to prevent this possible loss. The first meeting was held in January 1951, with a follow-up meeting in February, at which they decided to join with Feis Lar na hÉireann, a Gaelic League *feis* that was, for many years, held in Mullingar at the same time as the Fleadh Cheoil was held in the town over the Whit weekend. On 14 October 1951 the first standing committee of Cumann Ceoltóirí na hÉireann was elected at Arus Ceannt, Thomas Street, Dublin. At a meeting on 6

A group of musicians, singers and dancers who toured England and America.

January 1952 the name of the organisation was changed to Comhaltas Ceoltóirí Eireann. This was the beginning, and how the fledgling organisation has grown over the past fifty plus years!

It is now the biggest cultural organisation in Ireland, with satellite branches in America, Canada, England, Scotland, Wales, and even in Japan. Like the Gaelic Athletic Association, Comhaltas, as it is now known, has branches in every county in Ireland and the organisation has a pyramidal structure. Local branches are governed by a County Board, which in turn is represented at the Provincial Council, which in turn is represented at national level at the very top of the pyramid, at Comhaltas headquarters in Belgrave Square, Monkstown, Dublin.

Since 1951 the main event of the Comhaltas year is the 'gathering' at Fleadh Cheoil na hÉireann where musicians, singers, dancers, and followers meet at a given venue to play music, sing, and dance, to the delight and enjoyment of the assembled masses. Whether on a street corner, in an alley-way, a public house, schoolhouse or local concert hall, the music seemed to be never-ending. In the formative years of the organization, competitions were held as a means of testing the proficiency of the competitors in a particular instrument or grade, and they were not connected to the qualifying competition. This soon changed with competitions, grades and entries becoming very streamlined at county and provincial levels, culminating at national level with the All-Ireland Competitions. The 2001 Fleadh Cheoil in Listowel attracted over 230,000 people, including over 10,000 performers. The Fleadh Cheoil incorporates many aspects, including concerts, ceilithe, parades, pageants and street sessions – something to suit all tastes. In recent years television has played a big part in promoting the Fleadh Cheoil and all of its facets, particularly by looking back at previous Fleadhs through the eye of the camera, and these programmes contain great memories.

The aims and objects of Comhaltas are to promote traditional Irish music in all its forms: to restore the playing of the harp and uilleann pipes, to promote traditional Irish dancing, to foster and promote the Irish language at all times, to create a closer bond among all lovers of Irish music and to cooperate with all the bodies that work on restoring Irish culture. Comhaltas also aims to establish branches throughout Ireland and abroad to achieve the above-mentioned aims and objects. Well, it has to be said that Comhaltas has certainly gone a long way towards accomplishing these aims and objectives, especially in terms of the preservation of music. A very valuable archive of music and song has been set up at Cultúrlann na hÉireann, Comhaltas headquarters, where over 4,000 hours' worth of edited material is stored and is constantly being updated. It reflects the many talents and styles of the various regions of the country and the Irish community abroad.

Comhaltas has a number of traditional cultural centres throughout Ireland, including Brú Ború in Cashel, Cois na hAbhna in Ennis, Dún na Sí in Westmeath, Bruach na Carraige in Rockchapel and Dún Uladh in Tyrone for the promotion of the native culture. Educational facilities have a high priority in the Comhaltas programme, so numerous classes and courses are available under its auspices. In addition to over 600 music classes each week, other educational facilities are available to members and non-members alike, such as a diploma course for teachers of traditional Irish music, and Scol Eigse, a week-long summer college held annually in the week preceding Fleadh Cheoil na hÉireann. A nation-wide traditional Irish music examination in partnership between Comhaltas and the Royal Irish Academy of Music is available twice yearly, and a quarterly magazine, *Treoir*, keeps one up to date with all Comhaltas happenings and events, and even has some pull-out tunes in manuscript format. Comhaltas also has an interesting and informative website that offers great sound bites for visitors' appreciation at www.comhaltas.com, and is always worth a visit. In the hands of Comhaltas, our native music, song, and dance are safe and prospering. The house dances may be long gone, but so are the dance halls – and yet fiddles, flutes, pipes and melodeons are still churning out the music. Long may it last.